FORENSIC SCIENCE

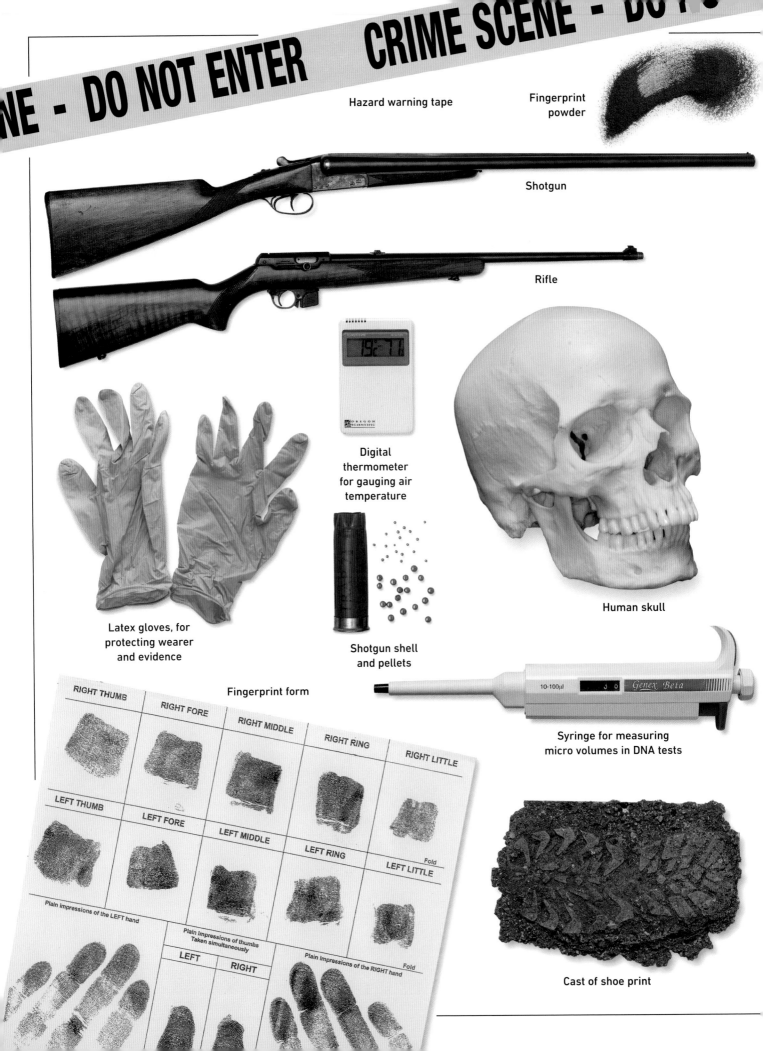

CRIME SCENE - DO T

NE - DO NOT ENTER

Hazard warning tape

Fingerprint powder

Shotgun

Rifle

Digital thermometer for gauging air temperature

Human skull

Latex gloves, for protecting wearer and evidence

Shotgun shell and pellets

Syringe for measuring micro volumes in DNA tests

Fingerprint form

RIGHT THUMB	RIGHT FORE	RIGHT MIDDLE	RIGHT RING	RIGHT LITTLE
LEFT THUMB	LEFT FORE	LEFT MIDDLE	LEFT RING	LEFT LITTLE

Fold

Plain impressions of the LEFT hand

Plain impressions of thumbs
Taken simultaneously

LEFT	RIGHT

Plain impressions of the RIGHT hand

Fold

Cast of shoe print

Linen tester for
magnifying
fingerprints

EYEWITNESS
FORENSIC
SCIENCE

Beretta 92FS
pistol

Written by
CHRIS COOPER

Forensic investigator's toolkit

Vial for DNA samples

Callipers for Bertillon body measurements

Sniffer dog

Photographer's marker card

Pipette

Scalpel

Tweezers

Fingerprint powder brush

Camera for photographic record

Magnetic wand

Sterile swab and container for sample

DK | Penguin Random House

SECOND EDITION
DK DELHI
Senior editor Shatarupa Chaudhuri Senior art editor Vikas Chauhan
Project art editor Heena Sharma Assistant editor Sukriti Kapoor
DTP designers Pawan Kumar, Nityanand Kumar
Picture researcher Geetika Bhandari Jacket designer Priyanka Bansal
Managing editor Kingshuk Ghoshal Managing art editor Govind Mittal

DK LONDON
Senior editors Anna Streiffert Limerick, Camilla Hallinan Art editor Chrissy Barnard
US editor Megan Douglass US executive editor Lori Cates Hand
Jacket design development manager Sophia MTT
Producer, pre-production Robert Dunn Producer Sian Cheung
Managing editor Francesca Baines Managing art editor Philip Letsu
Publisher Andrew Macintyre Associate publishing director Liz Wheeler
Art director Karen Self Publishing director Jonathan Metcalf
Consultant Dr. Clive Steele, Professor of Forensic Science,
School of Applied Science, London Southbank University

FIRST EDITION
DK LONDON
Consultant Dr. Clive Steele, London Southbank University
Project editor Mary Lindsay Art editor Neville Graham Photographer Andy Crawford
Managing editor Camilla Hallinan Managing art editor Owen Peyton Jones
Art director Martin Wilson Publishing manager Sunita Gahir
Category publisher Andrea Pinnington Picture researcher Sarah Hopper
DK picture library Rose Horridge, Emma Shepherd
Senior production editor Vivianne Ridgeway Senior production controller Man Fai Lau

DK DELHI
Art director Shefali Upadhyay Designer Govind Mittal DTP designer Harish Aggarwal

This American Edition, 2020
First American Edition, 2008
Published in the United States by DK Publishing
1450 Broadway, Suite 801, New York, NY 10018

Copyright © 2008, 2020 Dorling Kindersley Limited
DK, a Division of Penguin Random House LLC
20 21 22 23 24 10 9 8 7 6 5 4 3 2 1
001–317441–February/2020

A catalog record for this book
is available from the Library of Congress.
ISBN 978-1-4654-9372-9 (paperback)
ISBN 978-1-4654-9686-7 (hardback)

DK books are available at special discounts when purchased in
bulk for sales promotions, premiums, fund-raising, or educational use.
For details, contact: DK Publishing Special Markets,
1450 Broadway, Suite 801, New York, NY 10018
SpecialSales@dk.com

Printed and bound in China

A WORLD OF IDEAS:
SEE ALL THERE IS TO KNOW

www.dk.com

Contents

In pursuit of the criminal

FORENSIC SCIENCE IS THE USE OF SCIENTIFIC methods and knowledge to investigate crime—the word "forensic" comes from the Latin *forum* and means presenting and interpreting scientific information in court. Forensic scientists gather evidence from the scene of a crime and people's homes and workplaces that may link a suspect to a crime or prove him or her innocent.

Forensics at the crime scene
Forensic investigators must collect evidence as soon as possible after the crime, while it is still fresh—even if the area is unsafe. To protect the scene from contamination, they wear cleansuits, which prevent traces from their clothes or skin fouling the evidence.

This scientist prepares a blood sample.

In the laboratory
A scientist in a laboratory of the Federal Bureau of Investigation (FBI) searches for clues on a gun from the scene of a crime. She looks for clues such as fingerprints or traces of blood or sweat that might identify who last used the gun. She also looks for signs that the gun has recently been used, or marks that show where the gun was made.

A forensic scientist tests a gun for clues.

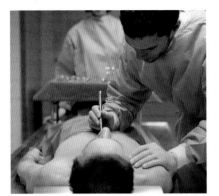

At an autopsy

A forensic pathologist's main job is to find out the cause of death and tell the police if there are signs of a crime. After checking the body for any external clues as to the cause of death, he cuts it open to examine the internal organs. He removes some for close examination, but they are all replaced in the body before it is buried or cremated.

Forensics in court

At a criminal trial, it is the job of forensic scientists to provide evidence, regardless of whether it favors the prosecution or the defense. When American football star O. J. Simpson was tried for double murder, the defense and prosecution lawyers pitted their own forensic experts against each other. The jury doubted some of the prosecution's evidence, and the trial ended with Simpson's acquittal in October 1995.

Forensic expert presents evidence.

Aerial photo of location of crime scene

Close-up view of evidence at the crime scene

FBI officer talks to the press.

Forensics before the public

Police rely on the forensic team to ensure any information that goes public is absolutely accurate. The forensic experts' reconstruction of a crime and the description of suspects will play a large part in the investigation and in the prosecution that follows.

Forensics as entertainment

Greg Sanders (played by Eric Szmanda) was a junior member of the forensic team in the hit TV show *CSI: Crime Scene Investigation.* Sanders used his enthusiasm for science to track down criminals. Despite criticisms of the ways in which the show often sensationalized forensic work, it is credited with creating unprecedented public interest in forensic science—as did the UK's *Silent Witness*— and has spawned *CSI: Miami* and *CSI: NY,* as well as many other programs worldwide.

Forensic anthropology

A forensic anthropologist can find out invaluable information about victims and crime by identifying and analyzing human remains. British professor Sue Black, for example, has worked on victim identification in wars in Kosovo, Sierra Leone, and Iraq, and natural disasters such as the 2004 Indian Ocean tsunami. More recently, she has set up a hand-recognition database, based on the unique individual anatomy of human hands.

Sliding arm of callipers to allow large measurements

The birth of forensics

In EARLIER TIMES, judges often thought they could tell suspects' guilt from how they behaved when accused or even tortured. Such ideas were gradually abandoned in Europe, and evidence was studied more systematically. In the 19th century, scientific advances made it possible to determine causes of death more accurately, microscope and chemical tests revealed more from evidence found at the crime scene, and measurements and photographs replaced rough verbal descriptions of suspects.

Alphonse Bertillon

Facial discrimination

An early attempt to classify human faces was made by Cesare Lombroso (1836–1909). He believed that some people are born criminal and that their faces give them away. He also invented the "lie detector" to measure heart rate—lying is believed to alter heart rate.

Cesare Lombroso

The poison man

Mathieu Orfila (1787–1853) was known as "the father of forensic toxicology" (the study of poisons). When a woman was being tried for murdering her husband with arsenic, which had been found in his food, Orfila found it in the man's body, too, and showed it had not come from the soil at the grave. The wife was jailed.

Mirror of the soul

Lombroso's book, *The Criminal Man*, shows a selection of faces that he believed typical of different kinds of criminal. No one now believes you can spot a criminal just by looking at a face.

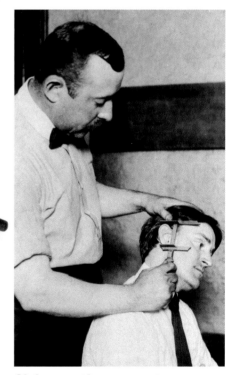

Sizing up the suspect

A New York police officer measures a suspect's ear in 1908. This was just one of dozens of measurements needed to build up a record according to the Bertillon system. If this man had committed any offenses in the past, or went on the run in the future, he could be identified—though not with total certainty—by his Bertillon measurements. This unreliable system was soon replaced by fingerprinting.

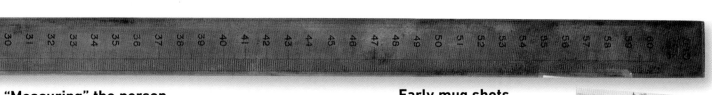

"Measuring" the person

The earliest scientific system for identifying people by their appearance was called Bertillonage, after its French inventor Alphonse Bertillon (1853–1914). It used measurements of the body, such as the lengths of arms and legs, the diameter of the head, and other statistics, as well as body markings such as scars or tattoos, and photographs of the suspect. The system could not always tell people apart, and suffered a blow in 1903 when Will West was sent to prison in the US, before it was discovered that another inmate there had almost the same Bertillon measurements—and was called William West.

Early mug shots

Bertillon measurements were supplemented with "mug shots," photographs usually taken from the side ("in profile") and the front. If the person committed a crime at some future time, his mug shot was distributed widely so that he could be recognized by policemen or the public. The profiles shown here are from just one of the many pages of Bertillon's original book of mug shots.

Window displaying recorded measurement

Rule measuring centimeters

Small sliding arm

Policing becomes scientific

This pioneering forensic laboratory was established in 1932 by FBI boss J. Edgar Hoover. Police forces began to realize scientific principles were needed in their work. The laboratory was equipped for up-to-date tests using chemistry, physics, and engineering. As scientific methods became more sensitive, so the precautions taken in collecting and storing the evidence became greater. Today, every major country has at least one advanced forensic science laboratory.

Fictional forensics

Sherlock Holmes, the fictional detective created by British author Arthur Conan Doyle, made his first appearance in print in 1887. Shown here with a magnifying glass and chemical apparatus, he is described as paying attention to tiny pieces of evidence that others have overlooked. The character of Holmes was (and is) wildly popular—this still is from the 1942 film, *The Voice of Terror*.

Basil Rathbone as Holmes

Letter from the Ripper?

This is one of hundreds of letters—probably all hoaxes—claiming to be from the serial killer "Jack the Ripper," who terrorized London's East End in 1888. Modern DNA testing suggests the letter is from a woman.

Securing the scene

IN THE PAST, policemen walked around a scene of crime and handled evidence with their bare hands. Today, at the scene of a serious crime, only authorized personnel are allowed past the police warning tape. The investigators record evidence on the spot, with photographs, sketches, notes, and measurements, and then take away essential evidence—including bodies if there are any. Speed is vital: witnesses are located and questioned while memories are still fresh, and physical evidence is preserved before it is altered by time or weather. This precious window of opportunity is known as the "golden hour."

By invitation only
One of the first things the police do when they arrive at the scene of a crime is make sure no one is in danger. Their next priority is to get help to anyone who has been injured. Then they cordon off the area in order to keep out onlookers and journalists until the evidence has been collected. This is to ensure that they do not accidentally contaminate the scene and mislead investigators. Only authorized police officers are allowed to cross the line.

One member of the team takes notes.

The forensic photographer makes a record of the scene.

Before a trail goes cold

If a body found at an incident shows signs of life, the person must be rushed to hospital. If not, it must be certified dead by a qualified medical examiner before it is moved. When Hurricane Katrina struck New Orleans in 2005, police couldn't assume that every body found was a victim of the hurricane and not of a crime.

First answer

Many investigations depend on a few facts among many thousands of items of information provided by people living near the scene of a crime. In the most serious cases, police ask everyone the same carefully devised questions from a checklist, and may be equipped with visual cues, such as photographs or drawings of victims or suspects.

Air crash scene

Crash investigators study the scattered wreckage of an airliner that caught fire on landing at Yogyakarta, Indonesia, in 2007. The cause of a disaster such as this is usually discovered only after a long and painstaking investigation carried out by experts at the scene. Many questions must be asked: was it an accident or a crime? Was the airline negligent, or was the aircrew careless? Did someone sabotage the plane?

Searching on hands and knees ensures no evidence is missed.

Fingertip search

A line of police officers wearing cleansuits advances on hands and knees, searching every square inch of a road. The body of a murdered woman was found nearby, and there could be signs of the killer's arrival or departure. Similarly thorough searches for clues may need to be made in the surrounding countryside, in streets, or through people's household waste. In many crimes, the searchers don't know what they're looking for. Although the vast majority of the objects found are not relevant to the investigation, they still have to be cataloged and treated as potential evidence until events prove they have no part to play.

Search patterns

There are many equally good patterns of search, but sticking to one ensures the best cover of ground in the least possible time. Directed by one person (to avoid confusion), the search should leave no area out, preferably cover each point twice, but not waste effort by searching the same area more than that.

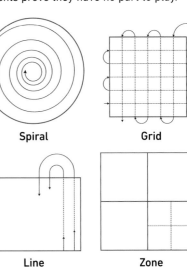

Spiral

Grid

Line

Zone

Recording the scene

Vital clue—dried blood on a brick

FORENSIC INVESTIGATORS make a permanent record of anything that might be relevant to the crime, writing down what they see, drawing diagrams, and taking photographs. This avoids having to rely on highly unreliable human memory, and provides evidence likely to be accepted in court. As French forensics pioneer Edmond Locard stated, "every contact leaves a trace"—from hairs, sweat, and flakes of skin to fibers from clothing or soil on shoes. Everyone at the crime scene wears protective clothing and footwear to ensure they do not contaminate the site.

Forensic fashion

The cleansuits worn by forensic officers prevent particles, fibers, sweat, and dirt passing from the investigators onto items of evidence. The scientists' work would be made much harder if the evidence they analyze included, for example, hair from one of the investigators, or soil they had tracked into the area. Cleansuits also help to prevent contamination if there is poison or infectious germs at the scene. Overshoes ensure the team's footprints are not confused with those belonging to the suspects.

Hood to keep hair in place

Face mask in case of noxious substances

All-in-one protective cleansuit

Capturing the scene

A forensic photographer records suspicious objects—such as this knife—at the crime scene, often with a scale to show the object's size. He photographs the crime scene from every angle, so that investigators do not have to rely solely on their memories or sketches when trying to reconstruct events at the scene.

Portrait of a crime

An investigator's drawing shows where a body was found, possibly the victim of a murder. The sketch also marks the positions of objects and the distances between them. A handheld computer may aid in rapidly producing a high-quality diagram. The sketch is signed as a true record of the scene.

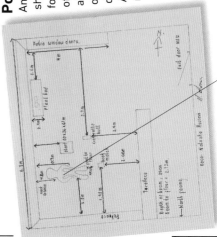

Position of body

Glove to protect skin and to preserve evidence from contamination

Equipment case

Overshoe

Sole of shoe marked "POLICE" in raised letters

Keeping track

Footprints have a short lifespan, but a copy, or cast, provides a permanent and transportable record. It is made by filling the print with liquid plaster of Paris or "dental stone" (used by dentists to make teeth molds). The low frame around the print seals off the area while the cast hardens. On an extremely soft surface such as snow, the print can be sprayed with a material that makes it firmer before attempting to make a cast of the print.

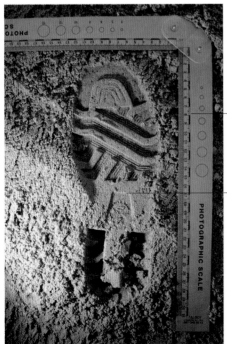

Footprint in damp sand

Scale to measure size of footprint

The shape of death

When a body is found at a crime scene, its outline is drawn on the floor if indoors or on the ground if outside. Only when the position of the body has been marked and the body photographed from many different angles can it be removed. Its position might give clues about an attack, or show that a suspect's story is not accurate. Any bloodstains nearby are also marked.

Plaster of Paris

Marker cards

Investigators place marker cards next to specific objects being photographed at the crime scene. The cards are numbered (or lettered) and a list is made so investigators, lawyers, and witnesses can later refer back to these objects and places with less risk of confusing or omitting vital information.

Card marking 15th piece of evidence

Static plate

Positioned as stepping stones, static plates are used whenever it is vital to avoid disturbing the ground or stepping on important clues.

13

Handling the evidence

An incident scene is a hive of activity as forensic investigators collect and record all evidence that could possibly be relevant. They must take great care that no one and nothing else can damage the evidence during the course of its life, which is often long. Each container of evidence is sealed, labeled, and signed so a court has confidence in its contents.

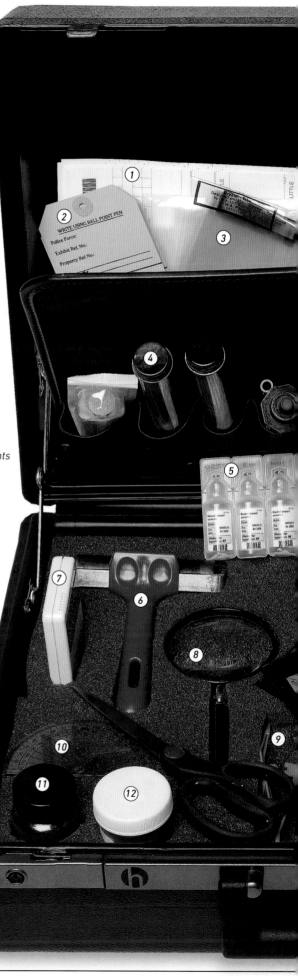

1. Fingerprint forms—
prints are inked onto these.

Toolkit

There is no time to lose at the scene of a crime or other incident—all the investigator's tools must be ready at hand. Evidence that needs to be preserved is put into bags, bottles, or envelopes. Blood and other fluids are gathered on swabs resembling cotton-tipped "buds." Containers are sealed, and labels track their movements. Used gloves and scalpels are disposed of to avoid contamination.

2. Labels *to attach to items of evidence*

3. Lifting tape *to "capture" fingerprints on objects*

4. Fingerprint brushes *for applying powder to fingerprints*

Photographic record

A digital camera is essential for recording a crime scene. Photos must be taken in a certain way, making sure the scale of each object is recorded accurately. A copy of the image is made, with the original file protected in custody as a safeguard against any image manipulation.

5. Vials *of pure water to dissolve dried stains*

6. Roller *for pressing lifting tape onto fingerprints*

Measuring scales

Forensic investigators measure objects at the scene to record their size in photographs and notes. These right-angled scales can be placed inside a corner—of a room, for example—or outside corners—of furniture, for example—to provide quick and easy readings.

7. Digital thermometer *measures air temperature at scene.*

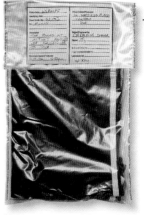

Bags of evidence

Every piece of evidence, large or small, must be placed in a tamper-proof evidence bag. Such bags may be made of paper with the contents hidden, or of plastic through which the evidence is visible, but all have a printed area in which every handler of the bag gives their details. This "chain of custody" ensures important evidence remains exactly the same as when it was first found.

Transparent evidence bag

8. Magnifying glass

9. Tweezers *to pick up small objects*

10. Protractor *to measure angles*

11. Aluminum fingerprint powder *to make fingerprints visible*

12. Magnetic fingerprint powder *to make fingerprints visible*

13. Disposable rulers

14. Swabs in vials *to collect samples of fluids*

15. Latex gloves

16. Measuring tapes

17. Scalpel, *a disposable knife*

18. Hazard warning tapes *to be placed around areas to be protected*

19. Pipettes *for moving drops of liquid*

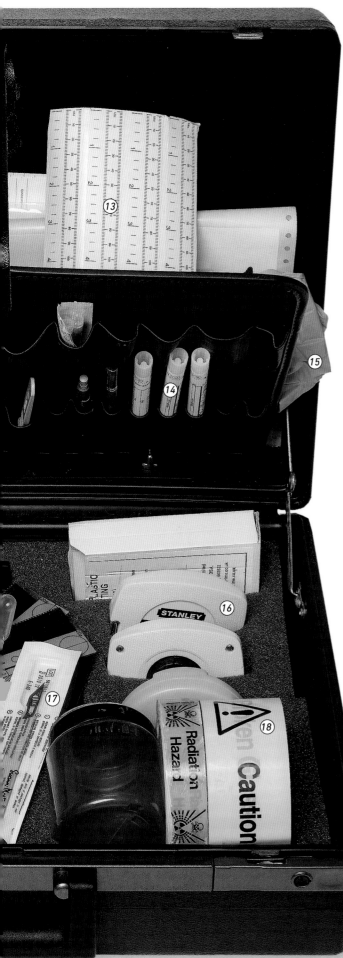

Paper evidence bag

POLICE EVI

Police Force
Identification Ref. No.
Court Exhibit No.
R-V
Description

Time/Date Seized/Produced
Where Seized/Produced

Seized/Produced By
Signed

Incident/Crime No.
Major Incident Exhibit No.

Laboratory Ref.

BAG OPENED BY
SIGNATURE
REASON
ADDITIONAL INFORMATION

Taking fingerprints

THE FIRST POLICE FORCE to systematically collect and store fingerprints to identify criminals was in Argentina, in the 1890s—today, every country has such a store. Forensic investigators try to find all the fingerprints at a crime scene. They make permanent copies of the prints and photograph them. Prints taken from everyone known to have been at the scene can be compared with those of suspects or people whose prints are held on file.

Dusting for prints
A police officer brushes fingerprint dust onto a car door. A smooth, metal surface readily takes fingerprints. Using fingerprint powder in a contrasting color helps show the prints. They might be found in an enormous range of places—the interior, exterior, engine compartment, trunk, and even underneath the car.

The wider view
The magnifying glass is one of the oldest and simplest aids for the detective, but still one of the most valuable. It is indispensable for getting a better view of fingerprints, significant marks and scratches, and small writing and printing.

Brushes
The fingerprint specialist uses brushes to cover areas where prints are visible or suspected with a fine powder. Sweeping away the excess leaves the pattern of the print revealed in the dust. A broad brush cleans larger areas; a narrower brush can be pushed into recesses. The type of brush also depends on the type of powder chosen.

Fingerprint powder
The consistency and color of the powder chosen depends on the type of surface being checked. Dark fingerprint powder usually consists of fine particles of carbon, rather like soot. Light powders may be chalk, titanium dioxide, or other materials.

Lifting tape
This clear adhesive tape can be pressed onto a surface carrying a fingerprint so that the print is transferred onto it. The print can then be removed for analysis and comparison with known prints on file.

Roller
A fingerprint roller smooths lifting tape onto a fingerprint. The pressure applied removes air bubbles and allows optimum contact between tape and print to make an accurate impression.

Procedure for taking fingerprints

Fingerprint specialists look for prints, produce a clear and accurate image of a print, and preserve it to be used as evidence, possibly years later. While LED forensic crime lights (see p.24) can reveal prints, brushing the surface with carbon powder is still a widely used method.

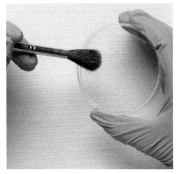

1 Brushing the surface
The prints on this dish are barely visible until an investigator (wearing gloves) brushes it lightly with fingerprint powder.

2 Revealing the print
A large print is now clearly visible on the surface. As a piece of evidence, it needs to be even clearer and more permanent.

3 Using the roller
Lifting tape is placed over the surface. As the roller smooths it down, the grease making up the print is transferred to the film.

4 Copying the print
The investigator peels the lifting tape away from the surface of the dish. The tape now carries its copy of the fingerprint.

5 Fate of the fingerprint
The print on the lifting film is placed in a protective sleeve with a label recording when and where it was obtained. The physical print is safely stored, and its details are filed in a computer database.

Waving a wand

A magnetic wand used with metal dust is an alternative to a brush used with nonmetallic powders. Some of the metal dust that forms a clump at the end of the wand sticks to the grease of a fingerprint pattern and produces a recordable print.

Magnetic
Magnetic powder contains iron so that it is attracted by magnets. It cannot be used on iron, steel, and many other kinds of metal.

1 Gathering dust
The tip of the wand is inserted into magnetic fingerprint dust. The dust forms a "brush" with little risk of damaging a print.

Magnetic tip attracts filings

Large magnetic wand   **Pen-size magnetic wand**

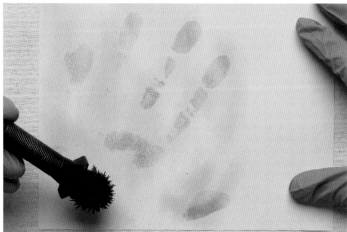

2 Making contact with the print
Gently brushing the magnetic dust over the surface reveals a large part of a hand. Normally only fingerprints are kept on file, but hand markings are also unique to each person and can be a useful addition to the evidence.

Analyzing fingerprints

Linen tester
This gadget is an alternative to a magnifying glass. It comes in different sizes and strengths of magnification and folds up compactly.

STUDYING THE PATTERNS of looped and branching ridges on fingertips, the British scientist Francis Galton showed two crucial facts: everyone's prints are different, and everyone's prints stay the same for life. Every country has records of fingerprints and police trained in collecting and analyzing them. Computerized databases allow fingerprint details to be flashed between police forces around the world in seconds. Palm prints and footprints are also unique, and sometimes these, too, are used to identify people, whether victims or suspects, alive or dead.

Sir William Herschel
In the mid-19th century, Herschel, a British official in India, got the local people to put their palm prints—and later just two fingerprints—on legal documents as a way of showing their agreement. He soon came to realize that fingerprints were unique individual identifiers.

Quick printing
Fingerprint specialists often use ready-inked pieces of film to speed up the process of taking fingerprints. When the protective layer has been peeled off, the witness or suspect presses each of his or her fingertips onto the ink. Each fingerprint is then transferred onto a specially printed fingerprint form.

Each finger of each hand has an individual and distinctive appearance.

Pre-inked paper has made print taking quicker and less messy.

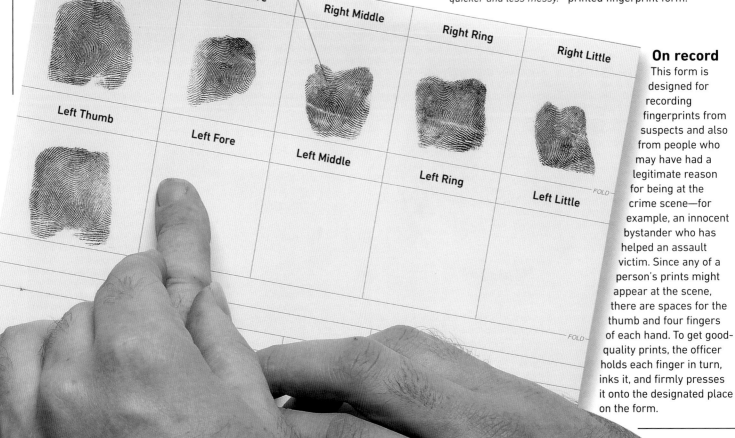

Right Thumb · Right Fore · Right Middle · Right Ring · Right Little
Left Thumb · Left Fore · Left Middle · Left Ring · Left Little

FOLD
FOLD

On record
This form is designed for recording fingerprints from suspects and also from people who may have had a legitimate reason for being at the crime scene—for example, an innocent bystander who has helped an assault victim. Since any of a person's prints might appear at the scene, there are spaces for the thumb and four fingers of each hand. To get good-quality prints, the officer holds each finger in turn, inks it, and firmly presses it onto the designated place on the form.

Patterns of prints

The three most common types of fingerprint are shown below. In loops (the most common), each ridge enters and leaves on the right or left side of the finger. In whorls, the ridges near the center of the pattern form closed curves. In an arch, each ridge enters and leaves on opposite sides.

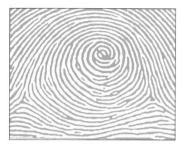

Whorl

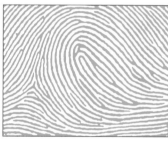

Loop

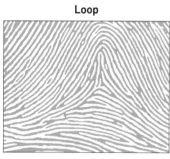

Arch

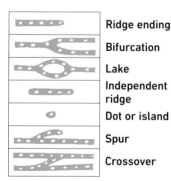

	Ridge ending
	Bifurcation
	Lake
	Independent ridge
	Dot or island
	Spur
	Crossover

Galton details

Named after the fingerprint pioneer Sir Francis Galton (1822–1911), the tiny distinctive details listed above appear on fingerprint ridges. If the expert comparing two prints finds many identical Galton details, both prints must come from the same person.

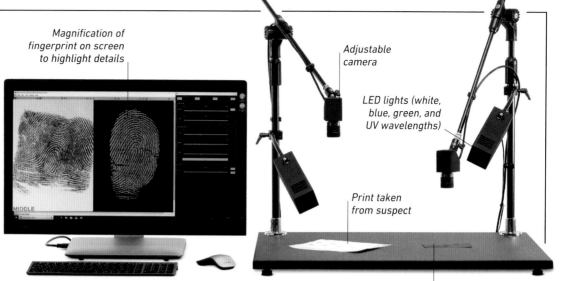

Magnification of fingerprint on screen to highlight details

Adjustable camera

LED lights (white, blue, green, and UV wavelengths)

Print taken from suspect

Print on object from crime scene

Matching the prints

To find out whether two fingerprints are the same, two images of the prints are placed on the comparator, which enlarges and projects them side by side on the screen. The expert looks for the main features—loops, whorls, and arches—and then at the Galton details—how ridges end, branch, or form tiny loops and dots. The main patterns are often crossed by cracks in the skin or tiny scars, which can change the print's appearance, so the expert disregards these.

Superglue fuming

To make faint fingerprints more visible, this helmet and drill are put in a cabinet with a glue-like substance. When heated, the glue gives off fumes that react with the grease in the prints to form a hard opaque deposit that is easy to see.

Shining a light on crime

Finding a fingerprint is one thing but getting a clear enough copy to be able to analyze it in detail is quite another matter. The fingerprints on this tin can have already been made clearer by the superglue treatment (see left), which has coated the can in a hard deposit. The next step of shining a laser rather than ordinary light on the can reveals the prints even more clearly. Then the prints will be photographed, and the can will also be kept as a permanent record until the crime is solved.

Fingerprint revealed by glue fuming

Computerized matching

A fingerprint expert compares the fingerprint image in his hand with two images on a computer screen. The handheld image is from the scene of a recent crime; the computer versions are from records of known criminals, stored on a database. The original analysis of the electronic prints after they were first taken was largely carried out by computer. Computers can store and quickly process a lot of data, but only the human eye is capable of confirming the final match.

Written in blood

In the past, blood was not a very useful clue in a crime. If a farmer's clothes had a suspicious stain on them, for example, he could claim it was an animal's blood. But in the late 19th century, chemical tests were invented that could show whether a stain was blood or not. Since then, ever more sophisticated ways of analyzing blood have been devised that show whether blood is animal or human, which blood type it is, and even how the person died— if, for example, by poison or suffocation.

Karl Landsteiner
Around 1902, an Austrian biologist and immunologist called Dr. Karl Landsteiner (1868–1943) showed that there are several types, or groups, of blood. In police work, if two bloodstains are of different types, it follows that they must come from different people.

Blood sample

Reagent (chemical used for testing)

John Glaister
A Scottish police doctor and professor of forensic medicine, John Glaister (1892–1971) classified bloodstains into six types, according to their shape, which depended on how they were produced. Much the same classification is still in use today.

Testing kit
Four rows show samples of the main blood types: A, B, O, and AB. Reagents have been added to confirm each blood type. In the left-hand column, anti-A reagent makes A and AB form a clot, which proves the existence of A antigens, but B and O remain liquid as they contain no A antigens.

Kastle-Meyer test
The quick blood tests that investigators can do at the scene of the crime are called "presumptive" tests. The most common is the Kastle-Meyer test. If the test indicates a stain or mark could be blood, more detailed tests will be carried out in a laboratory for confirmation. These will also reveal whether the blood is human or animal, what its type is, whether it shows signs of disease, and much more.

1 Removing a trace
A stain found on a brick at the site is suspected to be dried human blood. An investigator rubs it with the corner of a paper disk folded in four in order to collect a tiny sample.

2 Checking the sample
The disk is unfolded, showing the sample grains in a dot at its center. Gloves protect the sample from contamination and the investigator from disease-bearing fluids.

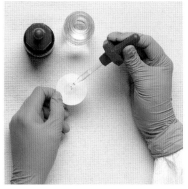

3 Adding a chemical reagent
The investigator adds a few drops of phenolphthalein from a dropper onto the sample. The test is so sensitive that only a small quantity of the chemical is needed.

Patterns of bloodstains

The shape of bloodstains can give valuable information about their cause: whether they came spurting from an artery or dripped slowly from smaller blood vessels; whether the victim was moving at the time; or whether the injury was caused by a blow, a knife wound, or in some other way. In the 1930s, Sir John Glaister classified bloodstains into six main types: drops, splashes, pools, spurts, smears, and trails. Since many factors can influence the shapes, an expert has to be cautious in their interpretation.

Blood is smeared over a large area.

Point from which blood trails radiate

Blood smear

The blood smear (left) is the result of a quantity of blood being spread over a surface, either by the injured person trying to get away from the scene, or by the person falling as he or she dies. A blood smear may also be caused by the victim being moved from or within the crime scene, either at the time of the injury or soon afterward.

Impact splatter

If a bloodstain found on the floor or ground splatters out from a central area (as shown above), it shows the blood fell from a height. Calculating how far it fell can yield information about the height of the victim, or his or her location when attacked.

Shoe print

In a violent incident, with much blood shed, no one is likely to leave the scene unmarked. Here, an excellent blood print from the sole pattern of a shoe has been left near the scene of the crime. The print gives clues to the size and make of shoe, and shows some defects that may link it uniquely to its wearer.

Teardrop shape

Blood stains are often teardrop-shaped. This is may be a result of a drop flying through the air and spreading as it strikes a surface. This can give valuable clues about the movement of the victim as he or she was wounded. In other cases, the teardrop shape is due to gravity forcing the blood downward.

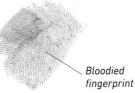

Circular drop

A circular shape indicates that the drop of blood struck the surface at right angles—usually by falling vertically onto a floor.

Fingerprint

A fingerprint in blood provides two pieces of evidence in one. But it is possible the print came from the criminal, and the blood from their victim—or vice versa.

Bloodied fingerprint

More blood on intact side of shoe

4 A second chemical

The investigator now adds a few drops of hydrogen peroxide. The two chemicals combined in the presence of even a minute quantity of blood cause an effect that is visible to the naked eye.

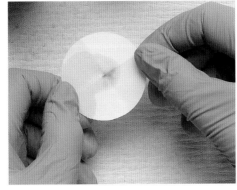

5 Blood revealed

The paper turns a bright pink where the stain has mixed with the two chemicals. This means the stain is likely to be blood. After confirmation, the sample will most likely be taken to a laboratory for more detailed tests.

Sole's wear and tear causes less blood here.

DNA analysis

DNA TYPING, or "genetic fingerprinting", has brought a revolution in forensic science. DNA (deoxyribonucleic acid) molecules are spiraling chains of atoms, packed into the center of every cell. DNA carries genetic (inherited) instructions about how our bodies are built, such as the color of our hair and eyes. Only identical twins, triplets, and so on share the same DNA. A single hair, a drop of blood, or a smear of saliva at the scene of a crime can reveal who the criminal was—provided the DNA is stored in a database and a match is made.

Sample to profile

DNA samples may be taken from the scene of a crime—for example, from a blood stain—and from suspects, usually taken from cells scraped from inside the cheek. A test can show whether the crime-scene samples come from one individual or more than one, and whether the suspect is the same person as the person at the scene.

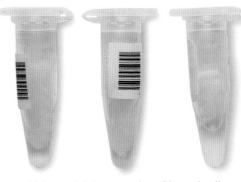

Scraper for collecting buccal (cheek) cells

Vials containing samples of buccal cells

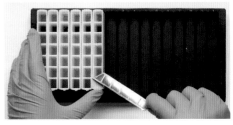

1 Transferring the DNA

A scientist takes a sample from the first vial and drops it into the first compartment of a multi-part container. Her pipette (dropper) measures the precise amount she drops in. She repeats the process for the first compartment in each of the six containers.

2 Preparing to purify

The first compartment of each container now holds a different DNA sample. The other compartments hold chemicals. A foil seal is peeled off the six containers, ready for the process to extract and purify the DNA.

3 Extracting and purifying

The machine will mix each DNA sample with the chemicals in the second compartment, then mix the results with the chemicals in the third, and so on, until only the DNA remains.

Pioneers of DNA

In 1953, Francis Crick (1916–2004) and James Watson (b.1928) discovered that DNA's molecule is in the form of a double strand. Each strand is a helix (similar to a spiral staircase) and consists of about 100 million chemical units (bases). Each base is a small group of atoms. A small fraction of the bases are "instructions" for the organism. The rest has no known function—but it's what is used in "genetic fingerprinting."

Sir Alec Jeffreys

Alec Jeffreys invented DNA typing, or genetic fingerprinting, in 1984. It was first used to investigate two murders committed in 1983 and 1986. A young man had confessed to both murders and had been charged, but he appeared to have the wrong type of blood. Jeffreys was able to show the two murders had been committed by the same person, but not by the man who had confessed. Eventually, the DNA evidence showed another man was the killer. In the first police use of DNA testing, Jeffreys had proved the innocence of one man and the guilt of another.

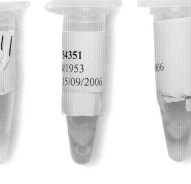

Comparing profiles

The DNA profile for each sample is the pattern made by selected fragments of the DNA that are spread out according to size. There are several ways to show this: the graphs below were produced by electrophoresis. No two people have exactly the same peaks, or spikes, in the same positions in such a graph.

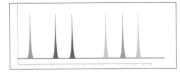

Crime sample
DNA from the scene is compared with samples taken from various suspects.

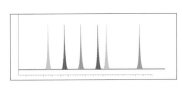

Victim sample
The victim's DNA may be at the scene, and must not be confused with the offender's.

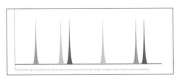

First suspect
This shows a different pattern of peaks from the crime sample. It can be ruled out.

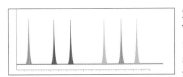

Second suspect
This DNA pattern matches the crime sample. This suspect was at the crime scene.

Endangered species

Parrots, hummingbirds, and many other birds of Central and South America are threatened by the illegal trade in exotic pets, and huge numbers die in transit. The authorities can analyze DNA from the remains of smuggled animals to identify the species and where the animal originally come from. If it belongs to a protected species, prison or a heavy fine can follow.

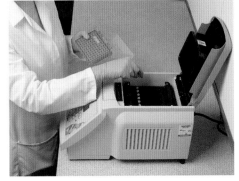

4 Amplifying the DNA
To ensure forensic scientists have enough DNA for their tests, this machine "amplifies" it (increases its amount) by running the samples through a multi-step process called PCR (polymerase chain reaction). PCR doubles the number of molecules at each step. After doing this many times, there may be hundreds of thousands of times as much DNA as there was to start with.

5 Creating the profile
Inside an electrophoresis machine, a strong electric field of hundreds of volts separates the fragments of DNA by size. The positions of the fragments are recorded electronically and used to generate patterns or sequences of numbers. These visible patterns form the DNA profile of the person from whom the original DNA sample came.

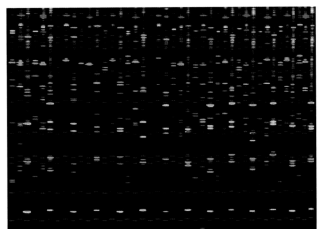

DNA profiles
The DNA profiles of several people are compared above. Even minute traces of a person's DNA can be displayed in this graphic way, for comparison with other samples. Increasingly sophisticated DNA databases around the world hold DNA records of offenders, whatever their crime or conviction. When a crime is committed, DNA from the scene of the crime is collected and compared with profiles that exist in the database—even for crimes committed many years ago.

Relatively guilty
In 2003, two men on a bridge threw bricks onto the traffic below. One smashed through a windshield, giving the truck driver a heart attack. Some of the criminal's DNA was found on the brick, but not in the national DNA database. The search was widened to look for similar DNA. A man on the database because of his criminal record had very similar DNA. His brother proved to be guilty.

Trace evidence

(see p.12)

FOLLOWING DR. EDMOND LOCARD'S exchange principle that "every contact leaves a trace" (see p.12), forensic scientists study some very tiny traces indeed—too small to see with the naked eye—using a range of advanced microscopes. Hairs that look identical when viewed with the naked eye may now reveal very different surface textures. Flakes of paint from a car consist of multiple layers, with differences in thickness and color— if a flake found at the scene of a crime matches a sample from a suspect car, it almost certainly came from that car.

Vacuuming up
A specially designed type of vacuum cleaner collects fibers, dust, and other trace evidence from furniture, carpets, curtains, clothing, and car interiors. The tiny nozzle reaches even the tightest corners.

Paint effects
A forensic scientist examines a sample of paint under an optical microscope and compares it with the vast range of samples in the foreground to identify its color and type (such as glossy or matte, oil- or water-based). With a scanning electron microscope (see right), an investigator can see much more.

Comparison microscope
Samples are best compared side by side so that differences and similarities show up clearly. Comparison microscopes present the two samples in the same field of view. This model has two built-in microscopes, each with its own light source. The images produced by each can be observed side by side through the center eyepiece, or on a connected computer screen. A camera attached at the top takes images to be kept for later analysis.

Camera attachment

Center eyepiece

Light source

Sample 1

Sample 2

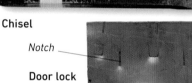

Chisel

Notch

Door lock

Tool marks
The metal plate above, part of a door lock, was damaged when an edged tool was used in a burglary. Detailed examination shows that the notches are the same width and thickness as the tip of a chisel owned by a suspect. By itself this doesn't prove the chisel's owner was responsible for the crime, but it can convince the police that they should investigate him closely.

Revealing light
Looking like a flashlight, a forensic crime light can reveal fingerprints, fibers, and traces of fluids and chemicals. It uses LED lights with a specific frequency band of light, usually in the visible spectrum, or just a little bit higher with ultraviolet (UV) or a little bit lower with infrared (IR). Special development chemicals are then added to bind with the invisible trace so that it can be seen and documented.

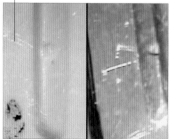

Tool mark shows nick in chisel

Suspect's tool mark   **Crime scene tool mark**

Tools compared
The far left picture shows a mark made by a chisel found in the possession of a suspect. This is compared with a mark found at the scene of the crime (near left). The investigator looks at the general shape made by the tool, such as the rounded bottom end, as well as individual distinguishing marks, in this case the nicks halfway along its length. Although similar in shape, the nicks are not in the same position. So the expert would conclude that the suspect chisel was not the one used in the crime.

Scanning electron microscope

Forensic scientists use scanning electron microscopes (SEMs) to study trace evidence. Unlike optical microscopes that use light to provide a magnified image, SEMs rely on a stream of electrons—when separated from their atoms, they form an electric current. In the SEM, the electron beam produces a highly magnified and very detailed image. Anything viewed under an SEM must be coated with metal so that the electric charge from the beam is conducted away. (If not, the charge builds up and interferes with the beam.) Here, a hair is stuck to a small metal disk, about $2/5$ in (1 cm) across, which is coated with a layer of gold in order to be viewed under the SEM.

1. Metal stub (small disk) for receiving sample hair

Adhesive film

Hair visible through gold

3. Gold-plated stub

2. Adhesive film holds hair in position

1 Preparing the evidence
The sample, attached to the small metal stub, is placed carefully in the chamber of the sputtering (plating) machine. The airtight lid is closed before turning on the machine. Air is pumped out of the chamber and a high voltage is applied. This creates a gold halo around the sample and gold deposits stick to the surface of the sample.

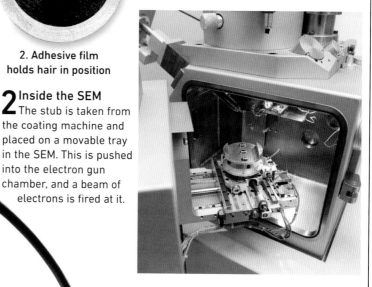

2 Inside the SEM
The stub is taken from the coating machine and placed on a movable tray in the SEM. This is pushed into the electron gun chamber, and a beam of electrons is fired at it.

3 Forming a picture
The beam of electrons is focused onto the sample by powerful electromagnets. The result appears on the computer monitor—a highly magnified, 3-D picture of the hair.

Chamber housing the electron gun that produces the electron beam

Sample chamber

SEM image of hair

Natural clues

THE AIR IS RICH WITH ALMOST INVISIBLE DUST. Powerful microscopes reveal tiny flakes of human and animal skin, hairs, grains of sand, soil, pollen, and even fibers from our clothes. So at any crime scene—including on the victim and the guilty person—there are many "invisible" clues that can be closely examined at a forensics laboratory. For example, it may be possible to identify the type and manufacturer of a carpet on the basis of a few fibers picked up at the scene and compared with a database of fibers, which might even solve the crime.

Slide show
Viewing specimens under a microscope, a scientist can tell if hair (top) is animal or human, and if fabric is synthetic (middle) or natural (bottom).

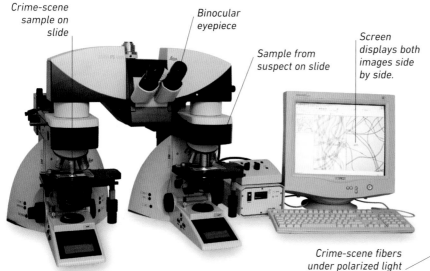

Crime-scene sample on slide

Binocular eyepiece

Sample from suspect on slide

Screen displays both images side by side.

Crime-scene fibers under polarized light

Comparing fibers
This advanced comparison microscope combines two microscopes. Two samples can be compared by observing through the binocular eyepiece, or on the computer screen. On the blown-up version of the screen (right), two synthetic fiber samples are being compared: one from the crime scene, the other from a suspect. If the samples are the same, they provide evidence—but not proof—that he or she was at the crime scene.

Looking at hairs
The color, type, and length of any hair found at the scene are all important clues, but an SEM (scanning electron microscope) can show individual aspects of the hair that are not visible to the naked eye. The hair in the upper image is clearly damaged. This could be due to excessive use of hair-care products, which would immediately exclude some people. In the lower image, the blue specks are particles of dried shampoo, which may or may not be significant.

Damaged hair shaft

Hair coated with shampoo particles

Looking at pollen
Under SEM, different pollen spores can be identified by their intricate structures. Since there are thousands of plant species with which to compare the image, it is not always easy to find the right one. Each type of pollen is produced at definite times of year, so pollen found in the clothing of a victim or suspect can give important clues about when and where they have been.

Ragweed pollen

Multifaceted pollen grain

Sunflower pollen

Getting it taped

An investigator presses tape onto a wool sweater and peels it off to collect loose fibers for analysis. The fibers may show where the wearer of the clothing has been, or who they have been in contact with. Sometimes tweezers are used for picking up single fibers, but tape is faster. Tape plus fibers can be stored permanently in case investigators ever want to take a second look.

Sticky tape pulled across sweater

Wool and unidentified fibers seen sticking to tape

Edmond Locard

Locard (1877–1966) was a leading French forensic scientist. During his lifetime, his famous exchange principle that "every contact leaves a trace" (see p.12) became more and more important, as scientific advances made it possible to detect even tinier traces at the scene of an incident.

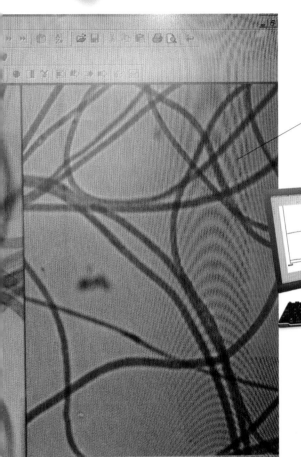

Fibers from suspect under polarized light

Graph showing the fiber's composition

Spectrometer's FTIR machine

Microscope's binocular eyepiece

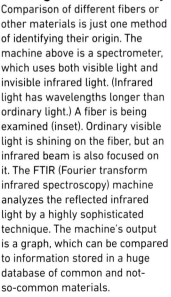

A sample fiber under visible and infrared light

Finding a fiber's identity

Comparison of different fibers or other materials is just one method of identifying their origin. The machine above is a spectrometer, which uses both visible light and invisible infrared light. (Infrared light has wavelengths longer than ordinary light.) A fiber is being examined (inset). Ordinary visible light is shining on the fiber, but an infrared beam is also focused on it. The FTIR (Fourier transform infrared spectroscopy) machine analyzes the reflected infrared light by a highly sophisticated technique. The machine's output is a graph, which can be compared to information stored in a huge database of common and not-so-common materials.

Seeds of suspicion

Grass seeds solved the murder of Louise Almodovar in 1942. She was strangled on November 1 in Central Park, New York. Her husband Anibale was held as a suspect. Grass seeds found in his pockets and trouser cuffs were identified by a botanist as a rare species—in New York, the grass grows only in Central Park, where Louise had been killed. Anibale claimed he'd walked in the park in September, but when told the grass produces its seeds in mid-October at the earliest, he confessed.

A good impression

IF THERE ARE FOOTPRINTS AND TIRE TRACKS at a crime scene, the investigators photograph them and possibly make a cast (a solid copy in hard material). The patterns of shoe prints are cataloged and kept on a computerized database. An officer notes the size of the footprint and the pattern of diamonds, curves, squares, and other lines on the sole. With these details, the brand, the date it went on the market, and a picture of the whole shoe can be quickly found. The same thing can be done with prints of tires—then a list of all vehicles that use that make of tire can be called up. Even scrapes and dents can yield vital clues.

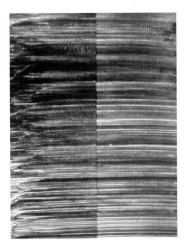

Bolt-cutter match
Every cutting tool leaves its own "fingerprint" (pattern of marks). The left-hand microscope image above shows marks left on a chain cut in a burglary. The right-hand image shows marks made in a laboratory by a bolt-cutter found by the police. The pictures line up exactly, showing that the same blade made both cuts.

Powerful flashlight

Additional light source

Ultraviolet light tube

Lifting footprints
Even if a footprint is just a faint mark consisting of dust, shining a powerful flashlight at an angle rather than directly onto the print will often reveal it. Other kinds of light can reveal different substances more strongly. Ultraviolet light, for example, makes some substances glow. The forensic scientist can make a permanent record of a dusty footprint that he can take away to examine more closely in a laboratory. First he lays a sheet of foil-backed plastic film over the print, and touches a high-voltage probe to the film. The electrostatic charge attracts dust from the print to the film, forming an impression that can be set with a spray.

Burglar's tools
Fingerprints and unique marks on the blades of a crowbar and chisel can give away their user's identity. Even the tiny fragments left after the tools' use can provide clues; for example, they may have come from another crime scene.

Chisel

Crowbar

Tire tracks
A track left by a vehicle tire could be a valuable clue, so a permanent record is made. A photograph will do, or a latex (rubber) cast made in the same way as a footprint cast (see p.29). The image can be compared with a database of tire treads to narrow down the type of vehicle and the date and place of its manufacture. In addition, unique wear marks may help identify the vehicle that made the track.

Database tracks are compared with those from the scene

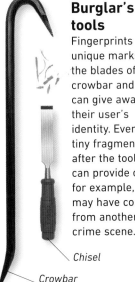

Rigid frame holds print in place.

Resin takes up shape of print.

Recording a shoe print

A footprint found at a crime scene is a valuable but temporary piece of evidence, so a cast must be made. First resin (a liquid plastic) is poured into the depression of the print. The liquid is left for a while until it sets (hardens) into a flexible, rubber-like solid. The pattern obtained is a negative of the shoe print—convex where the print is concave and vice versa—so a second cast needs to be made from this one, to show the true shape of the print.

Highly visible scale measures dimensions of print's pattern.

The second cast

A permanent record of the shoe print is made in the laboratory with a hard material such as plaster of Paris. Now the concave parts of the print are represented by concave parts of the cast, convex parts by convex. The pattern on this sole is clear but very common. Individual marks made by wear and tear will be unique to this shoe.

Patterns on sole may indicate brand.

Sole of suspect's shoe shows wear.

Measuring shoe prints

A forensic investigator measures the main dimensions of the heel and sole of a print and a suspect's shoe. These can be used to file individual records, in much the same way as fingerprints are stored in databases.

Measuring outline of shoe reveals its size.

Guns and bullets

FIREARMS CAUSE DEVASTATING HARM. At a crime scene where they have been used, officers quickly make safe any guns and ammunition that are present. Forensic investigators record the positions of the weapons and the damage caused by bullets to objects and victims. They search for the bullets themselves, and figure out the positions from which they were fired and the trajectories (paths) they followed. They also search for tiny particles called firearm discharge residue (FDR) or gunshot residue (GSR), which are blasted out by a gunshot.

Operation Trident
In 1998, London's Metropolitan Police set up a project, called "Operation Trident," which invited people to hand in guns and other weapons without fear of prosecution. Some of the guns had been used in violent crimes.

Twin triggers

Trigger guard

Stock

Rear sight

Foresight

Stock

Trigger

Magazine clip

Trigger guard

Safety catch

Rear sight

Hammer

Barrel

Slide

Foresight

Trigger guard

Grip

Trigger

13-round magazine within

Magazine release catch

Rifle
A rifle is a long-barreled firearm with spiral grooves called rifling inside its barrel. These make the bullet spin as it travels along the barrel, leaving characteristic marks on the bullet. A rifle often has a magazine clip, containing several cartridges (bullet containers). The user steadies the rifle's stock against the shoulder when firing. This, the long barrel, the rifling, and (sometimes) a telescopic sight all make the rifle a very accurate firearm.

Pistol
Pistols (handguns) like this Beretta 92FS—widely used by the military and police forces—are often called "automatics," but they are usually "semiautomatic": a single pull of the trigger fires the bullet, ejects the used cartridge, and readies the next cartridge for firing. When the gun fires, the top part (slide) is driven back. A spring then forces it forward again to load the next cartridge into the chamber. A fully automatic weapon can fire repeated shots while the trigger is pressed once and held.

Death in Dallas

The 1963 assassination of President Kennedy showed the lethal capabilities of powerful guns in criminal hands. The president was riding in an open-topped car through Dallas, Texas. Ex-marine Lee Harvey Oswald fired three shots from a sixth-story warehouse window. One shot killed the president.

The motorcade just before the shooting

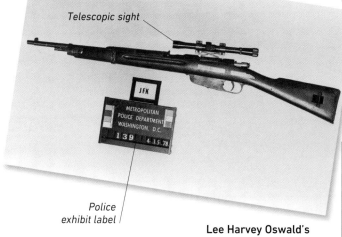

Telescopic sight

Police exhibit label

Lee Harvey Oswald's Italian military rifle

Shotgun

A shotgun is a long-barreled firearm that fires many small pellets (called shot) enclosed in a shell, rather than a single bullet. Unlike a rifle, the inside of its barrel is smooth. Its aim is less accurate than a rifle's, but this is made up for by the wide dispersal of the shot, which makes it easy to hit a target at close range. Criminals often like to carry shotguns during robberies to terrify people. A sawed-off shotgun has a shortened barrel, which reduces its accuracy. This weapon is favored by criminals because it is easy to hide in a bag.

Twin barrels for quick firing

Barrel

Plastic case

Metal head

Pellets

Power of the gun

Irrespective of shape or size, all guns produce an explosion that sends a bullet (or shot in shotguns) racing out of the barrel. In a rifle, the bullet is encased within a cartridge, together with gunpowder. A shotgun also holds cartridges, or shells, enclosing pieces of lead shot rather than a single bullet. With a pull of the trigger, the firing pin strikes and ignites the end of the cartridge causing the gunpowder inside to explode. This forces the bullet or shot out of the gun with great speed.

Rifle cartridge

A rifle cartridge is long and slim. The case is filled with gunpowder and the pointed bullet is on top. Made of lead, it is usually covered with a metal jacket.

Replica bullet

Although not designed to harm, a replica gun can be made deadly if the plastic pellet inside its bullets is replaced with a metal ball bearing.

Shotgun shell

A normal shotgun shell contains many pellets, called shot, instead of a single bullet. These do not follow an accurate path, but spread out after leaving the barrel. Shot can be of different sizes, described by a number—the larger the number, the smaller the shot.

Manipulated bullet

A "dum-dum" bullet is altered to do more damage when it hits a target. The bullet shown here has had the top of its metal jacket cut off, so that the jacket will spread when the bullet hits its target, causing a larger, more damaging wound at the point of impact or inside the body.

Modified bullet

Standard bullet

Replica bullet

Rifle cartridge

Pistol cartridge

A pistol's cartridge differs from that of a rifle. It is shorter and broader in relation to its length. After the bullet is fired, the empty cartridge is immediately ejected from the gun by the force of the explosive power. This same force brings the next cartridge into the firing chamber.

Lead bullet

Gunpowder explodes and forces out bullet.

Cartridge case

Primer ignites gunpowder.

Pistol cartridge

Firearms in the laboratory

THE STUDY OF GUN USE is called "ballistics." It covers the processes involved as the bullet is fired and travels down the barrel, and what happens when the bullet strikes the target. Chemical analysis of firearm discharge residue (FDR) with the aid of a scanning electron microscope (SEM) is also key.

Bullets and cartridges

A rifle cartridge is shown with two smaller pistol cartridges, beneath the lead bullet they each contain.

Ear covers, helmet, and eye shield protect shooter.

Test firing

A firearm of interest undergoes a test firing. It may have been found at the scene of crime, or in the possession of a suspect. After firing, the marks made by the gun on the bullet and on the cartridge are examined. If they match those found on bullets or cartridges left at the scene, the weapon and its owner are linked to the crime. New brands of gun are also tested, to catalog what marks they leave on ammunition. A bullet from a crime scene can then be checked and the weapon identified.

Bracket holds gun steady at a specific angle.

1 Firing bullet
Wearing protective gear, a forensic scientist fires a gun into a shooting bath filled with water. The bullet's trajectory is slowed down by the water inside.

2 Retrieving the bullet
The investigator drags out the fired bullets for microscopic examination. Then photographs of the marks made on the bullets by this particular weapon will be permanently stored in the computerized police database.

Shooting bath

The path of a bullet fired from a particular gun can be tested in the shooting bath. Water can stop a bullet in a surprisingly short distance.

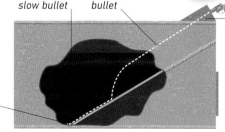

Water to slow bullet   *Path of bullet*

Gun bracket

Bullet at rest

Shooting bath

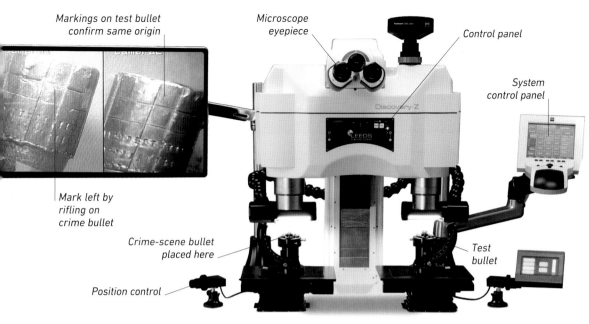

Markings on test bullet confirm same origin

Microscope eyepiece

Control panel

System control panel

Mark left by rifling on crime bullet

Crime-scene bullet placed here

Position control

Test bullet

Impact damage

A bullet is grossly distorted (above right) when it hits anything solid. A test bullet fired into a water bath (above left) is far less damaged, but the two can be compared for striations (grooves) and rifling on the sides of the bullet. These indicate which types of gun could have fired it, and the distance it was fired from.

Signature of a gun

A bullet from a crime scene is placed under a comparison microscope together with a bullet fired in the laboratory from a suspect weapon, in order to compare them at high magnification. Marks are left on the cartridge when it is forced into the chamber on loading, and by the hammer or firing-pin when it is fired. The barrel's rifling also leaves characteristic grooves along the length of the bullet. All these may show a link between a gun and a crime, but more evidence is needed—such as a matching type of gunshot residue or a DNA link—to prove that a particular person fired a particular shot.

Finding a cartridge

A forensic officer places a used cartridge into an evidence bag at the scene of crime, after marking and photographing its position. A criminal rarely has time to pick up used cartridges, so they are a frequent source of information.

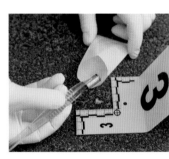

Comparing cartridge cases

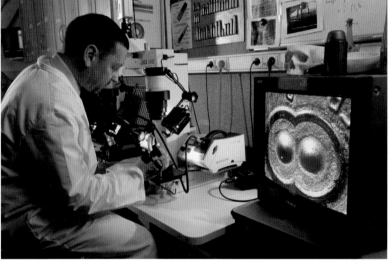

Two cartridges, one from a crime scene and one from a test firing, are being studied under a comparison microscope. Visible here are the rims at the rear of the cartridges, and the central percussion caps struck by the weapon's firing-pin. Both areas will carry unique markings made by that weapon. Under high magnification, similarities and differences between these markings help the investigator decide whether there is a connection between the two cartridges.

Condemned by ballistics

In 1920, two payroll guards were shot and $16,000 was stolen in Braintree, Massachusetts. Nicola Sacco and Bartolomeo Vanzetti were tried for the crime. A firearms expert showed that the markings on a test bullet fired from Sacco's revolver matched those of one of the fatal bullets. The men were executed in August 1927.

Vanzetti   Sacco

Deadly path

A policeman uses a rod to reconstruct the path of a bullet that struck this car. If a bullet hole is deep enough, a probe can be inserted to show the direction of entry. Tracing trajectories is especially important if more than one person was using a gun at the scene.

Probable position of gun

Rod links bullet hole with gun's position.

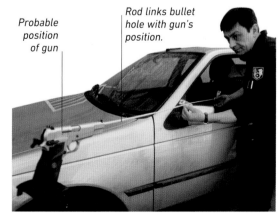

At the scene of the crime

A CRIME INVESTIGATION may be sparked not by a crime scene or a body but by a missing-person report. If a person is found dead, whether after a search or not, the first question is who are they, and the second is whether the death is due to foul play. Even a death arising in the course of a crime is not necessarily a murder. All the clues have to be collected that might help a court decide whether the death was due to accident, negligence, recklessness—or murder.

Sniffing it out

These sniffer dogs search the scene after a failed bomb attack at Glasgow Airport. Dogs also search for drugs and missing people—alive or dead. Springer spaniels (left) and other "cadaver dogs" are specially trained to scent a dead body, even if buried.

Cockpit provides 180° vision.

Eye in the sky

A police helicopter crew coordinates with police and volunteer searchers on the ground before continuing its flight in search of a missing person. Using a helicopter is a costly method of search, but it can cover a wide area and access areas that would prove difficult for land vehicles. That is why it is the equipment of choice in incidents involving the sea, lakes, mountains, moors, deserts, and other inhospitable terrain. It can also carry infrared heat detectors and other sophisticated devices capable of detecting a living or dead body from the air.

Who's who

In the aftermath of a shooting, the search to identify the victim begins. This clean-suited officer carries a stack of yellow position cards ready for placing by evidence, which will be photographed and stored for safekeeping. Documents and other personal effects found on or near the body are also cataloged, as they may help identify the victim, and friends or relatives may provide telling details. In this case, the victim was an innocent bystander who had intervened during an attack on two security guards.

The Body Farm

Dr. William Bass looks at a body donated by the deceased to the Body Farm—a research center in the US that studies how bodies decompose. Bodies are buried in different types of soil, or left out in the open or in the trunks of cars. Studying how the bodies decompose can help pinpoint time of death.

A triple killer

In December 1993, "Big Mike" Rubenstein reported finding three of his relatives dead in their mountain cabin. He had visited twice in November and found the cabin empty, he said. Body Farm scientists used their knowledge of how bodies decay to show the victims had died in mid-November. Rubenstein was lying, and was eventually convicted of the three murders.

Going deep

A diver searches a stream in a hunt for a missing woman—some of her possessions were found in the water close by. Often working in extremely poor visibility, divers are increasingly aided by sonar equipment, using high-frequency sound waves to generate an image of objects on the bottom. If this indicates objects of potential interest, divers go underwater to investigate.

Going underground

GPR (ground-penetrating radar) helps searchers when a body or other evidence is suspected to have been buried in a certain area. The GPR unit sends out radar (high-frequency radio) waves. These are reflected more strongly by some objects under the ground than by others. The image shows whether something unusual is present, then experts decide whether it is worth carrying out a more thorough search.

Police officer gives instructions to volunteers.

Underground details are relayed to monitor.

Net encloses blowfly
incubator, used to study
life cycle of insect.

A bug's life

WITHIN MINUTES OF A PERSON DYING, flies arrive, guided by substances released by the decomposing body. The flies are the first of many types of insects to set up home on the corpse. Some insects eat the flesh themselves, but most come to lay eggs. The young larvae that emerge from eggs and feed on the body grow at a fairly definite rate for each species. Waves of other insects arrive to feed on the larvae. A forensic entomologist (insect specialist) can often figure out the time of death from a study of the insects and larvae on a corpse.

Mite

Mites arrive soon after flies. They often eat the eggs and maggots of other insects.

Moving in

Insects colonize a body in a definite pattern: blowflies arrive first; rove beetles come at 4–7 days after death, closely followed by wasps; next come ants, cockroaches, and other beetle species at 8–18 days; clothes moths are among the final visitors, when most of the fleshy parts of the body have already been eaten. As a very general rule, if the only signs of habitation are eggs, death has probably occurred in the past 24 hours. At the other extreme, hatched adults at the scene suggest death happened two to three weeks earlier.

Springtail beetle

This late arrival can indicate the person died some time ago.

Wasp

Wasps usually feed on earlier insects, and may lay their eggs in the maggots on the body.

Blowfly pupae

Water for consistent humidity

Maggot farm

This net houses blowfly pupae growing on rotting meat in a forensic laboratory. Scientists study their rate of growth, the stages they go through, the effects of light and temperature, and the effects on insect development of drugs or alcohol in the meat—as in dead bodies. All this information is valuable when trying to figure out the time and place of a suspicious death. Investigators carry out a similar process of growing eggs, maggots, or pupae from the scene, to identify what insects are present and their stage of development.

Clothes moth

In the final stages of decomposition, this moth's larvae may feed on the hair.

Ants

Often found on and around a dead body, ants feast on the larvae and maggots of some of the other insects feeding from the corpse.

4 Adult

Two to three weeks after the blowfly's eggs were first laid, the fully formed adult flies emerge from the pupae. They have all the characteristics of flies, including six legs, a single pair of wings, and huge eyes. The adults do not feed on flesh— only the maggots do this. The time taken for the adult to emerge is strongly dependent on temperature— the warmer the surroundings, the faster the development.

1 Eggs

Each adult female blowfly that arrives at the corpse will lay about 250 eggs in the ears, nose, other openings, wounds, or folds in clothing—wherever it is warm and moist. The eggs are tiny—each egg measures only about $1/12$ in (2 mm) in length. It takes only about 24 hours for the eggs to develop into the next stage of the cycle—maggots.

24 hours

24 hours

Life cycle of the blowfly

Blowflies are a family of insects that includes many species. Some of these are the familiar metallic-looking bluebottles. All blowflies lay their eggs on the flesh of decomposing bodies, and also on open wounds. The first blowflies to arrive at a fresh corpse typically turn up within minutes. For this reason, the eggs, larvae, pupae, and adult forms of the fly found on a corpse are one of the best guides to the time since death. A forensic investigator will collect all the insect life he or she can see on or near the corpse and will grow them to maturity in the laboratory to identify them.

2 Maggots

A maggot is an insect larva that is blind and legless, but it is able to move by wriggling, and able to feed. Blowfly maggots in a corpse molt, or lose their skins, twice, to go through three larval stages, each bigger than the previous one. If the maggots cluster into masses, they generate heat and attract other insects that feed on them. The last maggot stage ends one to two weeks after the eggs were laid.

7–14 days (three larval stages occur)

3 Pupa

In this stage of development, the blowfly turns from a shapeless maggot into the adult fly. The maggot first develops a hard casing, or puparium. The transformation from larva to adult takes place hidden inside this apparently lifeless casing. The pupa cannot move or feed, and lives off food stored in its body. It spends as long as a week in this state. Then the newly developed fly forces its way out.

7 days

Maggots give the game away

The charred remains of a man were found in a burned-out car, 18 days after he'd been reported missing. The live maggots on his body were judged to be 2 days old: had he been dead for only 2 days? In his brain, there were also dead maggots. These had developed for about 14 to 16 days before they had died in the fire. The investigators concluded that the man had been killed soon after his disappearance. Two weeks later, the criminal had tried to disguise the cause of death by burning the car with the body in it. Insects returned to colonize the cooled body.

A burned-out car can initially disguise the cause of death.

Cause of death

A POST-MORTEM (after-death) examination, or autopsy, begins with an external assessment of the body by a forensic pathologist. He or she looks for signs of injury and—with stab or bullet wounds—studies the angle of impact and the depth of penetration. If the initial examination indicates suspicious circumstances, the pathologist will open up the body for further clues. Finally, the body is sewn up so that it can be buried or cremated.

Autopsy room

A body that has to be examined is brought from the mortuary (see p.39) to an autopsy room. Here a pathologist will piece together the facts behind a suspicious death. The body is placed on a specially designed stainless-steel table and cleaned. Hygiene in the autopsy room is of utmost importance, both to protect the pathologist's health and to ensure the evidence is not contaminated. Any organs removed are weighed, since an abnormal organ weight may indicate the cause of death.

Refrigerated cabinet for storing body parts

Raised lip prevents liquids from spilling onto floor.

Scalpel

Bone cutters

Hand saw

Tools of the trade

A pathologist's work ranges from making large cuts through flesh and bones, which requires a saw and bone cutters, to small cuts and removing tiny pieces of tissue, which requires a scalpel. Removing and sampling the brain involves yet further specialized tools, including the brain knife and cranium chisel.

Brain knife

Cranium chisel

Autopsy procedure

To open up the body, the pathologist uses surgical saws to cut through bone, and surgical tools to cut out and into each organ. The procedure follows a set sequence. First to be pulled out are the esophagus (gullet) and stomach. Then out come the heart and lungs, followed by the brain. Finally, the liver and kidneys are removed.

1 Y-incision
A Y-shaped cut is made across the chest and down the body.

2 Open the chest
The flesh is peeled back to reveal the ribs and soft organs.

3 Access to organs
The front ribs are removed so that internal organs can be removed.

Examining the brain

The top of the skull is removed and the brain is first studied in position. Then the organ is removed and weighed. It can be preserved in formalin until it is returned to the skull for burial.

Scales for weighing organs

Chalk board for recording weights of organs

Autopsy table slopes toward drain at far end.

Water to clean body and wash away fluids released by autopsy

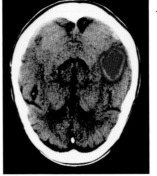

Death in the brain

A major cause of death in violent crimes is a hemorrhage (bleeding) inside the skull, after a blow to the head. If there are no outward signs of injury, pathologists open the skull to look for evidence. Brain scans can reveal hemorrhages (shown in red here) without opening the skull, but are mostly used on living people.

Cut to the bone

Stab wounds can be so severe that they penetrate deep enough to damage the victim's bones, leaving clear marks. Pathologists can sometimes link these wounds to a particular weapon, because imperfections in the blade match the marks it left on the bones.

Groove made by knife blade

Fragment of thigh bone

Tissue analysis

After an autopsy, a laboratory analyzes tissue samples from the various organs. Blood is tested for its type, and to see what diseases the person might have had. Testing hair can reveal whether and when the person took drugs. The key test is DNA typing (see pp.22–23), which can be carried out on almost any tissue or body fluid.

Autopsy record

Before a body is cut open, the pathologist usually draws a diagram showing all notable features—birthmarks, moles, tattoos, and so on, as well as any wounds, bruises, or other external markings that may possibly be linked to the person's death. Photos can also record body marks, but still need to be interpreted and annotated by the pathologist. Often a pathologist will record an audio commentary, detailing all the findings during the examination, so that later analysis does not have to rely on half-remembered facts.

Notable features marked on standard autopsy diagram

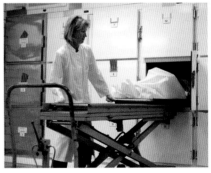

The mortuary

Dead bodies are kept in a storage room called a mortuary, or morgue. Each body is kept in a body bag in a separate large drawer. If an autopsy is needed, or if the person has not yet been identified, the body is kept chilled to avoid any further decomposition until burial or cremation.

Toxic world

IF DRUG USE OR POISONING is suspected in a crime, samples from an autopsy or crime scene may be sent to toxicologists, who test them for toxins—any substances that are harmful, or poisonous, to the human body. Whether legal or illegal, any drug can be toxic, even fatal, if taken in excess or used for the wrong purposes. As well as looking for toxins in bodies, forensic scientists also investigate toxic hazards produced by our way of life. Industrial wastes are often toxic, and new and poorly tested materials can pose health risks.

Warning—poison!
Emblazoned on pirate flags long ago to instil fear in their enemies, the skull and crossbones symbol is still used today to warn of deadly danger. Seen on a chemical bottle, or on the door of a cabinet or room, the skull and crossbones means that there is poison—a toxic substance—inside. The implications of this traditional and universal symbol are understood by the public around the world.

Environmental crime?
Not all crime victims are human. A scientist studies the corpse of a rare Indian white-backed vulture killed by a toxin. This might have been a result of criminal activity—farmers deliberately putting down poison to protect their animals from predators, or a factory negligently releasing a harmful waste product. In fact, this vulture and many others seem to have been killed by feeding on the carcasses of cows that had been given diclofenac, a veterinary drug.

Anthrax attack
On September 11, 2001, hijacked airliners crashed into the World Trade Center in New York City and the Pentagon in Washington, D.C. Nearly 3,000 people were killed. One week later, another terrorist attack against the United States began. Five letters containing spores of the deadly disease anthrax were sent to news companies and two US senators. Five people died, and 17 others were infected. Millions of dollars were spent trying to trace the source, decontaminate dozens of office buildings, and screen mail to prevent future anthrax attacks. The spores must have been prepared in a laboratory—and the type involved was first prepared at a US research laboratory in the 1980s—but the source was never identified and no arrests were made.

A forensic scientist checks a suspect package.

One of the letters containing anthrax

A classic murderer
When the remains of Cora Crippen, the missing wife of Dr. Hawley Harvey Crippen, were found buried in his basement, he was already on board a ship bound for Canada with his lover. The fugitives were spotted by the captain and arrested when they arrived in Canada. Crippen was found guilty of poisoning his wife and was hanged in November 1910.

Testing for toxins

Even a tiny amount of some toxins can be deadly. One of the most sensitive instruments for analyzing small quantities of a substance is the mass spectrometer. Molecules of different substances have different masses. By separating the molecules according to their mass, the spectrometer reveals which substances the sample contains.

1 Injecting the sample
A small amount is put in the mass spectrometer. Electron beams knock electrons out of the sample, turning its molecules into electrically charged particles called ions.

2 Pinball science
A strong electric field fires the ions up the machine from the bottom left-hand corner, and a magnetic field bends them around the curved track. Different substances' ions have different masses, so they take different paths, and separate out by the time they reach a detector bottom right. A graph will show any toxins present.

Poisons

Historically, poisoners could make it look as if their victim had died of natural causes. With today's sophisticated toxicology, few criminals could hope to get away with murder using any of the three poisons below. But accidental poisonings occur and forensic scientists may be called in to investigate.

Mushroom
Just one of many deadly types of fungi, the death cap mushroom causes an agonizing death with cramps, vomiting, diarrhea, delirium, and liver failure.

Strychnine
This plant's toxic leaves cause a very unpleasant, slow death. Violent convulsions lasting some time eventually cause exhaustion and lung paralysis, which leads to suffocation.

Antimony

This metal was once ground up and used in powdered form as a poison. Its distinctive metal taste is hard to disguise, so it would be given in small doses over a long period. Ultimately it caused death by heart failure.

Illegal drugs
Some drugs, such as heroin, cocaine, and amphetamines, cause serious harm and are prohibited by law—as is alcohol in some countries. If taken in large enough quantities, or with other drugs, they can produce life-threatening symptoms. If there are no signs of injury in a dead person, a toxicologist may test for evidence of drugs in the blood.

Cannabis
The most commonly used drug cannabis (marijuana) is illegal in many parts of the world. It can cause abnormal behavior, so victims and suspects in apparently motiveless crimes are often tested for cannabis.

Killed by ricin

Walking in London one day in 1978, Georgi Markov felt a jab in the back of his leg. He turned to see a man pick up a fallen umbrella, apologize, and jump into a taxi. Three days later, Markov was dead. The umbrella was a weapon that had injected him with a tiny metal pellet containing the deadly poison ricin. Markov was a political dissident from Bulgaria, and he was almost certainly assassinated by a Bulgarian agent.

Drilled hole to hold ricin

Actual size of pellet ●
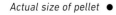

Heroin
Extracted from the opium poppy plant, heroin is a highly addictive drug and is commonly abused. Accidental overdose often causes death in addicts. Toxicologists can determine from a blood test whether heroin was responsible for the death.

The bones of the matter

Bare bones
From these human remains, reduced to mere bones after burial, the investigator will almost certainly be able to tell the sex of the person, and the height and age when he or she died. The ethnic group and state of health, and possibly even the cause of death, may also be revealed.

PHYSICAL ANTHROPOLOGY is the study of how the human body varies among different peoples around the globe. Forensic anthropologists assess bodies for evidence, and deal mainly with the skeleton—the part of a body that lasts longest when it's buried. Not only do people's skeletons change throughout their lives, but skeletons also differ according to sex—the pelvis (hip bones) is wider in a woman to allow for childbirth. In addition, skeletons vary around the world according to their ethnic origin. Forensic anthropologists sift through all this information to construct an accurate picture of the person whose bones they are investigating.

Ethnic comparison
A skull's shape can hint at a person's likely ethnic origin. Other clues come from the cheekbones, eye sockets, and angle of the face, as well as the nose bridge, nasal opening, and teeth. But this evidence isn't conclusive, as there are wide variations within each ethnic population, and people may have mixed ethnic origins.

European skull
Skulls of people of European origin are not as deep as those of African origin, nor as broad as those of East Asian origin. The face is also relatively flat.

Less deep (front to back)

African skull
Skulls of people of sub-Saharan origin are deeper than those of European ethnic origin. Cheekbones are lower, and eye-sockets are wider.

Wide space between eyes

East Asian skull
Skulls of people of East Asian origin are long, and broad in relation to their depth, with rounded eye sockets. Incisors (front teeth) are shovel-shaped.

Broad forehead

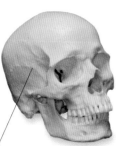

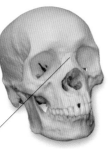

Mass graves
United Nations forensic scientists dig at a mass grave in Kosovo. In the late 1990s, civil war raged between the Serbian government and Kosovo, whose people are mostly of Albanian descent. The investigators try to reunite the bodies' scattered bones to find out who the victims were (or at least which ethnic group they came from) and how they died.

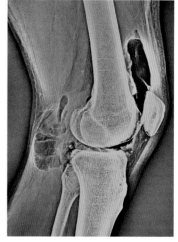

Arthritic knee
This X-ray of a knee joint shows little space between the bones—a sign of osteoarthritis, when cartilage wears away, so bones rub together and get damaged. After death, this person might be identifiable from medical records describing their condition.

Reconstruction of head in clay

Photo of missing man

From the ashes
In 1987, a fire swept through the underground railroad station at King's Cross in London. The identities of the 31 people who died were soon pieced together—apart from one man. Forensic sculptors reconstructed what they thought he had looked like from his fire-damaged skull. It was 15 years before the family of a homeless man connected him with the event and matched his photo to the restoration.

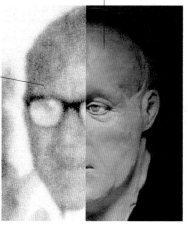

Waking the dead

The clay reconstruction shown here was made by a forensic sculptor from the cast of a young female's skull found in 1989 in Wales. The finished model was so lifelike that when it was published by the police, the victim was immediately identified by her social worker.

Cast of well-preserved skull

Face starts to take shape

Pegs inserted by modeler

Clay added to full depth

Clay built up on skull

Hair added

Facial features assumed

Shape of nose is guessed at.

1 Depth pegs
Pegs are positioned to show the typical depth of facial flesh and muscle on women of the same age.

2 Adding muscles
Clay is built up around the temples and jaw, representing the muscles and flesh in those areas.

3 Skin and nose
When the pegs are all covered, clay is smoothed over the whole skull, representing the skin.

4 Hair and complexion
The biggest guesses are made in the final stages, when adding the hair, skin color, and expression.

Computer modeling

Facial reconstruction is increasingly being done by computer, using data from CT (computer tomography) scans of living people. A CT scan of a head shows not only the skull shape, but also the depth of the overlying flesh. To "flesh out" the skull of an unknown person, the computer fits a CT scan around a digital model of the skull. Once facial details such as skin, eye color, and hair have been added, the reconstruction can be sent out to police forces and the media.

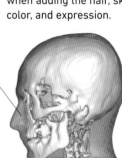
Facial tissue fits neatly over the skull shape.

4 Added extras
After the CT skull is warped and merged with the model, the computer adds the CT scan's flesh and muscle tissues (blue).

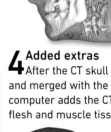

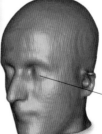
Head resembles a clay model.

5 Solid result
The computer generates a 3-D, 360° view, then details of eyes and hair are added.

1 Scanning a skull
A skull of an unidentified person rotates in front of a laser scanner, which sends data about its shape and size to a computer for a digital model of the skull.

Computer uses the landmarks as reference points when attaching the CT scan.

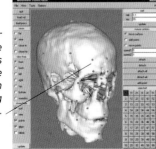

2 Preparing the model
The computer marks approximately the "landmark" points where a CT scan will be fitted to the digital skull, and a skilled operator fixes their precise position.

3 Best fit
A CT scan of a suitable skull is chosen from the computer's database, based on the forensic evidence for the sex, age, and race of the unknown person. The scan (red) is superimposed on the model (blue) to show where it needs warping (distorting) to fit.

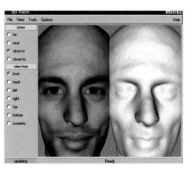

6 Back from the dead
For skin detail, a photo of a living face is wrapped around the model, which now looks more lifelike.

Spitting image

WHEN A CRIME HAS BEEN COMMITTED, getting a good picture of a suspect or a victim is vital. A likeness can be circulated to police officers and published in the media and online, recruiting the public in a bid to find a criminal or identify someone whose remains have been found. Police check any security cameras in buildings and streets in the area. If no pictures are available, or none of sufficiently good quality, a picture of the criminal's face will be made from witness descriptions. People struggle to describe faces in words, but can usually judge whether a picture resembles a face they have seen. Originally, police artists made drawings based on those descriptions, but today's computers can build up images with far greater accuracy. Voice analysis is another cutting-edge method that may aid identification.

Faces in a box

A photographic identification kit invented in 1968 was a great advance in getting descriptions of suspects from eyewitnesses trying to recall a face they may only have glimpsed. Facial features were sorted into a set number of types and then put onto photographic cards. The inventor, Jacques Penry, called his system "Photo-Fit." It was capable of creating 15 billion different faces. This box contains dozens of different choices for each facial feature, such as hair, eyebrows, eyes, nose, and mouth.

Facial jigsaw completed

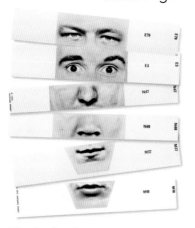

Photo features

The "identikit" system is made up of photos of facial features on strips of card (above). Witnesses are shown cards for, say, the nose. They pick the one closest to the nose they remember. This is assembled with other facial-feature cards to make a composite face (below left).

Finding potential matches

If a good image of a suspect has been provided, the computer speeds up the task of searching through records to see whether information on the suspect has already been gathered. Here, the image of a suspect appears on the left-hand side of the computer screen. On the right are 20 images selected by the computer as good matches to the suspect's photograph—it finds matches in just seconds from a database that may contain millions of faces. Then a human expert compares the selected images to see if any of them really do depict the suspect.

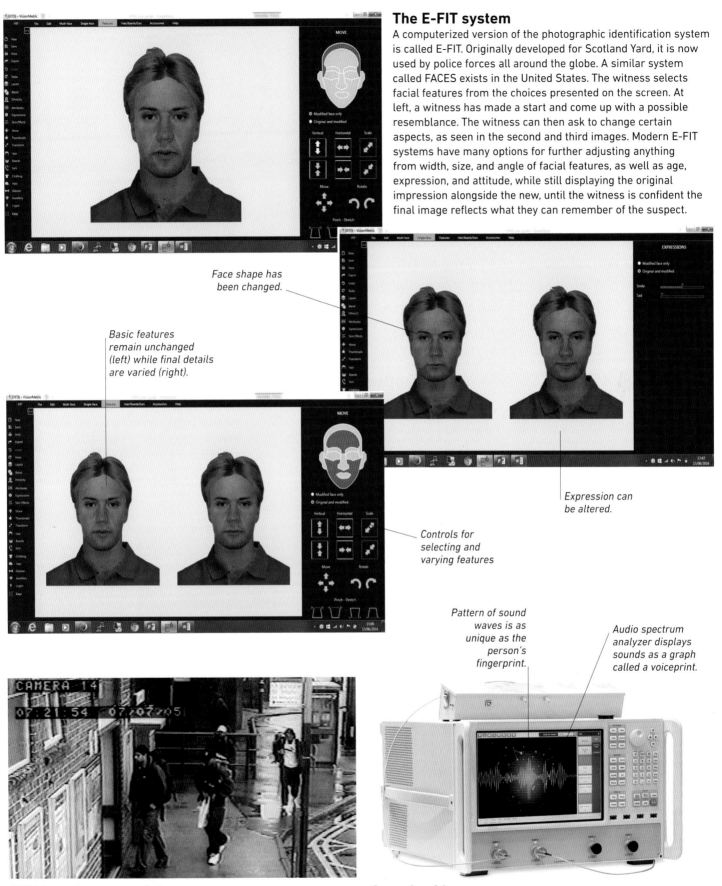

The E-FIT system

A computerized version of the photographic identification system is called E-FIT. Originally developed for Scotland Yard, it is now used by police forces all around the globe. A similar system called FACES exists in the United States. The witness selects facial features from the choices presented on the screen. At left, a witness has made a start and come up with a possible resemblance. The witness can then ask to change certain aspects, as seen in the second and third images. Modern E-FIT systems have many options for further adjusting anything from width, size, and angle of facial features, as well as age, expression, and attitude, while still displaying the original impression alongside the new, until the witness is confident the final image reflects what they can remember of the suspect.

Face shape has been changed.

Basic features remain unchanged (left) while final details are varied (right).

Expression can be altered.

Controls for selecting and varying features

Pattern of sound waves is as unique as the person's fingerprint.

Audio spectrum analyzer displays sounds as a graph called a voiceprint.

CCTV catches terrorists

These four inconspicuous-looking men had bombs in their knapsacks, which would kill them and 52 others in London. This and other CCTV pictures provided vital clues to their movements and terrorist network.

Sound evidence

Each of us has a unique voice. Speech experts can deduce our age, sex, and race by listening to voice recordings. To identify individuals, they may also compare "voiceprints" produced by voice spectrography.

Behavior of the offender

PROFILERS STUDY CRIMES to get a picture of the criminal's personality or way of life. Geographical profiling studies the locations and timings of a series of crimes. Burglars, for example, rarely commit robberies close to their own homes, and only do so at evenings and weekends if they have a legitimate daytime job. Psychological profiling studies the way the crime is carried out to deduce the criminal's personality and history. Someone who commits violent repeated assaults is likely to have displayed a violent personality in the past and have a police record. Though rarely accepted in court, the results of a "lie detector," or polygraph, test can indicate when someone is nervous or lying during interrogation.

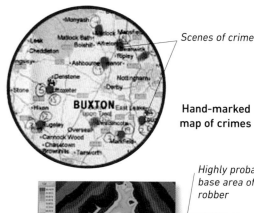

Scenes of crime

Hand-marked map of crimes

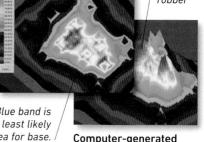

Highly probable base area of robber

Blue band is least likely area for base.

Computer-generated maps of probabilities

Getting warmer

Red dots mark a series of bank robberies in central England (top). An expert in geographical profiling mapped the probable location of the offender's base—his home or where he stored loot. Red areas are the most likely, blue the least. The profiler reduced the search area to a tenth of the area covered by the crimes, and the criminal was soon caught.

Jewelry robberies

An FBI map shows the locations and dates of a string of related jewel robberies along the East Coast of the United States that began in April 2003 and continued for some years. In total, more than 50 thefts occurred, amounting to more than $5 million in stolen jewelry. Creating a map like this is the first step in searching for behavior patterns that might reveal the perpetrators' base, means of transportation, and perhaps where they will strike next. Even with a smaller number of incidents, this type of map can be helpful.

Enfield, CT (2 stores) - 5/4/05
Guilderland, NY -3/22/04
Middletown, NY 6/13/03 & 5/17/04
Johnson City, NY - 5/15/03
Horseheads, NY - 9/1/03
Wilkes-Barre, PA - 9/14/05
Niles, IL - 8/3/05
York, PA - 11/13/05
Du Bois, PA 11/19/05
Sandy TWP, PA - 1/29/05
Monroeville, PA - 11/10/04
Allentown, PA (2 stores) - 10/3/05
Montgomeryville, PA - 12/5/04
Hagerstown, MD - 4/25/05
Eden, NC - 8/4/04
Concord, NC - 8/13/04
Pineville, NC - 8/22/04
Raleigh, NC - 4/3/05
Lithonia, GA - 10/3/04
Augusta, GA - 10/10/04
Bal Harbour, FL - 3/9/05
Miami, FL - 3/8/05
Boca Raton, FL - 3/9/05
Ft. Lauderdale, FL - 3/9/05

Manchester, CT - 5/2/04
Manchester, NH - 9/2/05
Nashua, NH - 8/15/05
Auburn, MA - 4/20/04
N. Attleboro, MA (2 locations) - 6/20/05
Waterford, CT -12/7/03
Providence, RI - 4/15/04
Warwick, RI - 1/14/04
Wallingford, CT - 9/11/05
Milford, CT - 2/22/04
Lake Grove, NY - 6/19/04
Hicksville, NY - 4/13/03
Huntington Station, NY - 8/30/04
Garden City, NY - 4/24/03
Massapequa, NY - 4/7/04
Bensalem, PA - 10/14/05
Abington TWP, PA - 1/13/05 & 10/17/05
White Marsh, MD - 8/9/03
Edgewater, MD - 3/20/05
Gaithersburg, MD - 4/10/05
Alexandria, VA - 5/27/03
Arlington, VA - 10/29/04
Springfield, VA - 10/8/03
Fredericksburg, VA - 7/28/03
Richmond, VA - 2/6/04
Colonial Heights, VA - 4/5/05

Forensic psychologist

Police may listen to a profiler's views, but they keep an open mind. They rarely work on "hunches," but use a trained forensic psychologist to help plan a methodical approach to catching the criminal and interview suspects. A forensic psychologist may also be useful for interviewing eyewitnesses whose memory recall might be affected by their emotional state and the passage of time.

Detecting lies?

A man is interviewed as he sits hooked up to a polygraph, or "lie-detector." Sensors record his pulse, blood pressure, breathing rate, and amount of sweating—both when he answers "neutral" questions (such as what he had for lunch) and when he is asked about the offense. Higher pulse rate, sweating, or blood pressure indicate nervousness and perhaps guilt.

Tubes record breathing.

Fingertip sensor measures sweating.

A profiling success

In 1956, Dr. James A. Brussel, a psychiatrist, drew up a profile of the "Mad Bomber" who had been terrorizing New York for years. He said the bomber was neat and tidy, a heavily built male, 40–50 years old, with a serious illness. He perhaps lived with an older female relative. And he might be wearing a double-breasted suit. The police eventually arrested George Metesky (right) at the house where he lived with his two older sisters. He fitted the profile, even wearing a double-breasted suit to go to the police station.

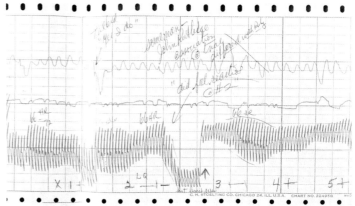

Portrait of a killer

Jack Ruby was a nightclub owner in Dallas, Texas, in the 1960s. He was also the man who killed President Kennedy's assassin, Lee Harvey Oswald. Investigators wanted to know his motive and whether he was part of a gang. His polygraph test (above) was examined for signs of untruthfulness in his story. He died before conviction.

Cuff on arm measures blood pressure and pulse.

Readings from "loaded" questions are compared with output from neutral questions to detect contrast.

Fire starters

WHEN A FIRE HAS THREATENED LIFE or actually killed, forensic investigators begin with two main questions: how did it start, and how did it spread? Deliberately starting a fire is called arson, but the great majority of fires start accidentally. The investigators try to find out how the fire progressed once it started, and whether dangerous materials played a part. A material that easily catches fire is said to be flammable. A fire might spread rapidly if a building has been badly designed, so forensic scientists have to keep up to date with the latest developments in building design and materials, since sometimes these can create new fire hazards.

Aftermath of fire
This room has been devastated by fire. Heat and smoke have destroyed the windows and furniture. If anyone has died, forensic scientists will investigate to decide how the fire started, and whether someone did it deliberately or was reckless or negligent. The electric heater in the center will interest investigators.

Sniffing for clues
After a fire, a forensic investigator will search for traces of accelerant—a fluid used to make fires burn more fiercely, such as petrol, paraffin, and turpentine. Handheld devices using infrared spectroscopy can analyze any gases picked up, but a sniffer dog, especially trained to detect accelerants, is often more sensitive than any instrument. If traces are found, a detailed examination of that area begins, and samples are taken to a forensic laboratory for thorough analysis.

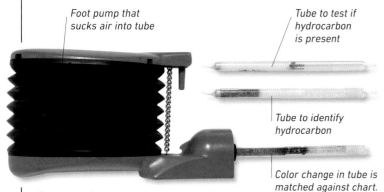

Foot pump that sucks air into tube

Tube to test if hydrocarbon is present

Tube to identify hydrocarbon

Color change in tube is matched against chart.

Gas analysis
This device for analyzing gas samples at the scene of a fire is called a Draeger tube. It consists of a foot-operated bellows that sucks air through a transparent tube containing chemicals. Different accelerants cause different color changes at various points along the tube.

Fire training
Firefighters are trained to recognize signs that warn of imminent trouble. This fire, started artificially in a training area, has reached a dangerous point, called "flashover," in which snakes of flame (right) begin to separate from the main fire. Forensic fire investigators must do part of their training in simulators like this in order to understand how fires work.

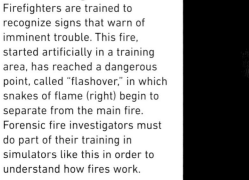

Not spontaneous
Experts believe that "spontaneous human combustion" (bursting into flame with no apparent cause) is in fact due to an unconscious person getting caught in a fire that starts in a normal way.

A burned-out building

Many buildings near the Buncefield oil depot were destroyed in the blaze (right), including this house. The total destruction of its interior shows how ferocious, all-consuming, and fast-spreading a fire can be. Although the forensic investigators know the cause of this fire, it is still their responsibility to look for signs that might indicate how and why it spread so far from the main site and why the consequences were so disastrous.

Towering inferno

A vast column of smoke is seen here rising from a burning oil depot at Buncefield, UK, in 2005. Described as the biggest fire in Europe since World War II (1939–1945), it began when automatic equipment overfilled an oil tank with gasoline, which then flowed into an open reservoir. A large cloud of gasoline vapor built up over the unmanned site, and the inevitable explosion engulfed more than 20 large storage tanks. No one was killed, but 2,000 people were evacuated, and the oil depot was devastated. Soon, forensic scientists established the sequence of events and ruled out terrorism.

Smoke plume rose nearly 2 miles (3 km) high.

Some fires were extinguished, but others were allowed to burn themselves out.

Fire testing

FIRE INVOLVES A COMPLEX CHEMICAL REACTION. When a material burns, it combines with oxygen from the air. Heat is released and new substances are formed. These include smoke, ash, and invisible gases such as potentially lethal carbon monoxide, hydrogen cyanide, and sulfur dioxide. People are killed by the heat, by poisonous gases, and by choking smoke—dense smoke also reduces visibility, hampering their escape. Forensic laboratories do a huge amount of work to investigate how materials burn, which materials are dangerous because they combust readily or give off toxic gases, and how buildings can be improved to lessen the risk of fires such as the one that rapidly engulfed Grenfell Tower in London in 2017, killing 72 people.

How did it start?
Samples of charred debris collected from a fire scene may yield valuable evidence. They are usually examined for traces of accelerant, which would suggest that the fire was a criminal act of arson.

Piece of charred carpet from fire scene

How much smoke?
Smoke is a killer. The smoke density chamber tests the smoke-producing properties of materials used in furnishings and construction. A sample, such as a piece of carpet, is mounted on a stand (inset). The heating unit glows with increasing heat, and the machine records the time it takes for smoke to be given off by the heated sample and to build up to a maximum. It also measures the amount of smoke produced, by detecting how strongly it absorbs light.

Sample mount

Controls

Sample glowing red-hot

Heating unit

Test chamber

How much heat?
The cone calorimeter (heat measurer) is a machine that tests the amount of heat energy materials give out when they burn, and the rate at which it is produced. This is important, because the more heat the material gives out, and the quicker it does so, the more intense the fire is and the faster it spreads. The calorimeter subjects a sample to extreme heat until it ignites. A computer then calculates how much energy is released by combustion, and how rapidly.

1 Preparing the sample
Here, the material being tested in the cone calorimeter is a type of plastic. A square sample of the plastic is placed on aluminum foil to be mounted in the machine. The foil will reflect heat from the cone onto the sample.

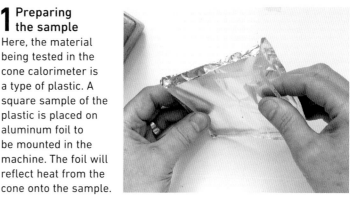

2 Positioning the sample
The sample is inserted under the electrically heated cone. A shutter then opens to expose the sample to the cone's intense heat.

3 Igniting the sample
As the plastic's temperature rises, it gives off hot gases, which are then ignited. Sensors detect the energy released.

How easily does it burn?

The oxygen index apparatus measures a material's flammability (how readily it burns) in terms of the amount of oxygen it needs to ignite. As a fire burns, it uses up the oxygen in a closed space, such as a room or a hallway. At the same time, the temperature rises—if it rises high enough, most materials will catch fire, despite the drop in oxygen. Scientists use a number scale—the oxygen index—to describe flammability. The lower the index number, the less oxygen the material needs to ignite, and the more dangerous it is to use in buildings, furnishings, clothing, and other products.

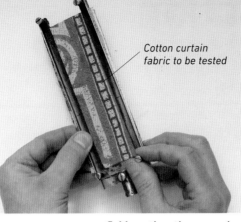

Cotton curtain fabric to be tested

1 Mounting the sample

This piece of cotton fabric is being mounted on a holder ready for placing in the machine. Other types of material can also be tested—the plastic coating of electrical wires, for example.

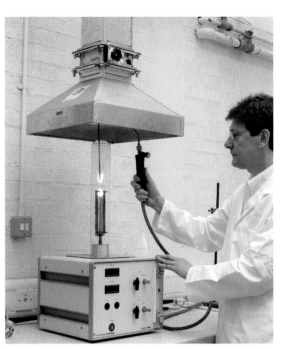

2 Igniting the sample

The sample is placed inside a strengthened glass tube. Hot air containing a controlled amount of oxygen is piped through the tube. The technician lights the sample with a curved gas lighter. Above the sample is the extractor hood—a chimney that sucks waste gases out of the tube.

Hood extractor draws off waste gases.

Lighter

3 Burning the sample

At a sufficiently high temperature the sample will burn, even in oxygen-poor air. The machine records the minimum oxygen content needed for combustion—the material's oxygen index number. Cotton, for example, has a relatively high index number of about 18, meaning it can burn in air that contains 18 percent oxygen—normal air is 21 percent oxygen.

Burning sample

Control panel

Crash investigation

A MAJOR INCIDENT IS ALMOST ALWAYS followed by a thorough investigation. A train, plane, ship, or several cars may be involved, and a large number of people hurt or killed. Whether the cause is accident, carelessness, or sabotage, the job of the forensic experts is to piece together the whole chain of events leading up to the disaster. They're helped by event recorders—"black boxes"—which are fitted to airliners, trains, and ships. These hold instrument and voice recordings of everything that goes on in the vehicle's control center.

Emergency stop
The lengths of skid marks, together with a knowledge of the vehicle type and how heavily it was loaded, indicate the speed at which the vehicle was traveling. If skid marks start on the wrong side of the road, they may indicate reckless driving.

Retrieved fuselage confirms bomb damage.

Early part of skid mark beginning to show swerve

Crash dummy
Car safety features are tested using crash dummies like the one shown here. The results are used not only in building safer cars but also in learning what the results of crashes are, so that forensic investigators can work backward from the aftermath of an accident to what actually happened.

Warning to unauthorized personnel

Signals in/out

Power supply meter

Reflective stripes to aid recovery

Crash-resistant case

Last words
Although called "black boxes," twin flight recorders are always bright orange, and tough, to make them easily visible in wreckage. This one is a Cockpit Voice Recorder (CVR), which records conversations among the crew. The Flight Data Recorder (FDR) stores data from the plane's instruments.

Pan Am Flight 103

On December 21, 1988, a Boeing 747 airliner, Pan Am Flight 103, exploded above the small Scottish town of Lockerbie. All 259 passengers and crew were killed, as well as 11 Lockerbie residents. After painstakingly reassembling the shattered pieces of the plane, forensic scientists discovered that a bomb placed in the hold had torn the plane apart.

Air accident investigator

Off the rails

In 1998, a German train was involved in a catastrophic crash near Eschede. There were 101 dead, and 88 seriously injured. Forensics revealed that a wheel rim had broken due to metal fatigue—a problem foreseen by other train operators, who had altered the design. As the train traveled over a set of points, the wheel hit a trackside lever, changing the points and derailing the rear carriages. The carriages hit a bridge, which fell onto the train. In complex cases like this, blame and responsibility can be difficult to establish.

The big bang

INSIDE A BOMB, a chemical reaction generates very hot, high-pressure gas that suddenly blasts outward, potentially devastating anything nearby. A typical bomb contains an easily detonated explosive, called the primary explosive. This triggers a more powerful but harder-to-detonate material, called the secondary explosive. A bomb can be made even more deadly by putting it in a tough casing, such as an iron pipe, or by packing shrapnel (nails or other pieces of metal) around the explosive.

Bus bombing
This double-decker London bus was wrecked by a bomb exploding at the rear of the top deck. The bombing was the last of four that took place in London on July 7, 2005. Forensics work established that the bus bomber was among the 16 dead, and that the explosive hidden inside his knapsack consisted of homemade materials.

Fragment of suitcase lining

Sniffer dog
A dog trained to detect explosives alerts its handler to a suspicious trash can. Sniffer dogs like this are taught to sit or bark when they encounter something that smells of explosive. The dogs are more efficient than any sniffer machines developed so far.

CMS   10   20

Suitcase bomb
These fragments of a suspect suitcase from the wreckage of Pan Am 103 (see p.53) were meticulously gathered and numbered along with thousands of pieces from the plane. After extensive study, investigators decided that the bomb was hidden in a cassette recorder inside this suitcase, which was stowed in the plane's hold. Fragments of the electronics of the recorder and labels on shreds of clothing led them to two men who were eventually charged with the crime.

Thwarted mission
A bomb placed in a vehicle is hard to detect. These large canisters of gas were removed from a truck that was intended to cause death and destruction in a city in Colombia, South America. The canisters are very strong, to keep the liquefied gas under high pressure. So the bomb included an extra explosive that was capable of cracking the canisters.

Back of bus
peeled apart

Bomb belt

Suicide bombers are hard to detect—a bulky jacket may be the only warning. Imitating a device worn around a suicide bomber's waist, this dummy "bomb" is being used in a training exercise for security guards. The real bomb would be triggered by a switch held in the wearer's hand. A guard attempting to make the bomb safe has the problem of immobilizing the bomber instantly, without giving him or her a chance to trigger the device. Since the bomber is prepared to die carrying out the attack, intercepting him or her with force may have little effect.

Improvised bomb

In this hastily constructed bomb, a liquid explosive is stored in the two aluminum flasks. The assembly is wrapped in plastic held together with sticky tape. Wires to detonate the bomb lead into the cylinders from the circuit board, but are here partly disconnected. A radio signal, most likely from a mobile phone, would have set off the electronic switch that triggered the bomb. A sophisticated trigger mechanism like this often gives more information than any other part of the bomb about the makers.

Flask containing liquid explosive

Part of detonating device

Trap for the unwary

The explosive, called Semtex, is on the left. Wires lead to a radio receiver on the right, to which a signal is sent to detonate the bomb. Disposal experts spotted that opening the box would have set off the mousetrap in the center—which would have triggered the bomb.

Radio receiver

Semtex

Mousetrap acts as a booby trap.

Countdown

A bomb sits in this plastic box, strapped to a bottle of gasoline. On the side of the box is a kitchen timer, which controls the time of detonation. The explosive inside the box scatters the gasoline and ignites it, making this a potentially devastating incendiary (fire-starting) device.

Bottle of gasoline

Circuit board triggers bomb when mobile phone signal is received.

Computer forensics

PEOPLE OFTEN MAKE FRIENDS, do business deals, and buy goods through devices connected to the internet. But crime is expanding fast in this digital world, on the regular world wide web and on the encrypted dark web. Vast sums are stolen. Young people can be drawn into danger by adults posing as teenagers. Terrorists share their knowledge of bomb-making. But cyberspace is not as anonymous as we may think. Police can find the rough location of a computer user who is visiting a suspect site, or the position of a mobile phone. Everyone leaves information about themselves whenever they shop or travel. The forensic investigator can take advantage of this electronic trail when trying to track down criminals.

The Pentagon hacker

Computer users across the globe attempt to hack (gain unauthorized access to) the computers of the Pentagon, headquarters of the US armed forces (above). In 2005, the US military claimed that the biggest hacker attack in history—on 97 Pentagon computers—had been carried out by Gary McKinnon (right), a computer administrator in Scotland. He claimed that he hadn't been interested in military secrets— he only wanted to find out what the US government knew about UFOs.

Phone user connects to nearest base station

Microwave dish links to other MTSOs

Base station

Person calling

MTSO

Person called

Mobile phone network

Mobile phone (or "cell phone") companies divide the area served into a grid of hexagonal "cells." Each base station (relay mast) is located at the point where three cells meet. Two people communicating are each connected to their nearest base station. Base stations communicate through an MTSO (Mobile Telephone Switching Office) to other base stations. The phone company's log shows investigators which base stations were involved in the call, and therefore which cells the callers were in, but not their precise locations. Mobile phones can also be tracked using GPS, without any call being placed.

The dark web

The dark web is used to make sure the identity of users is concealed. Information or items can be bought using a untraceable currency such as Bitcoin. Usually such items are illegal or controlled. Like the world wide web, the dark web is a global network allowing transactions between people across the world. It is difficult to penetrate for the police. Law enforcement agencies need to cooperate across international borders and keep up to date with the latest methods in order to investigate and solve this type of cyber crime.

Computer detective

A police expert removes the hard disk from a suspect's computer. Investigators follow a standard procedure when raiding computers, to avoid inadvertently destroying evidence. Special software is used to access data held on smartphones and laptops, although incriminating files may be held in cloud storage on special servers rather than on the device itself. The police will sketch or photograph the computers' positions and connections before removing them, and look for written notes containing passwords.

A virus strikes

A computer virus is a malicious software that replicates itself by modifying other computer programs and inserting its own code. Viruses can cause all sorts of problems with running software applications and can even cause a laptop to be unusable. Thousands of viruses are in circulation via the internet or shared USB drives. Computers can also be attacked by other types of malware known as "trojans" and "worms." Trojans are usually linked to ransomware where the victim is asked for money to stop any negative outcomes.

Cyber security

Computer-based serious organized crime and attacks on the strategic computer infrastructure via the internet by individuals, groups, and rogue states is a serious threat to countries around the world. In the UK, the headquarters of national cyber security organization is the GCHQ. The powerful computers housed in the doughnut-ring structure are able to look at huge data flows and target specific elements of the UK's internet. Interventions are carefully controlled so that the rights of UK citizens to privacy and freedom are maintained.

Smart card

A credit or debit card can "remember" data about its user. Its microchip or microprocessor—a tiny, complex computer circuit—encrypts data (translates into a secret code) for utmost security. On top of the microchip is the larger printed circuit, which connects to ATM terminals and card readers. The microchip can carry information about the cardholder's identity, bank balance, borrowing allowance, and so on. If the card falls into the hands of criminals, they will only be able to access the information if they also get the user's PIN (personal identification number).

Printed circuit connects with outside world

Front of plastic card

Microprocessor or "brain" of card

Glue

Plastic support

Recess

Card holder's account number

Paper trail

FORENSIC SCIENTISTS OFTEN NEED to make a close examination of a paper document. If it is a blackmail letter or threatening note, an expert may compare samples of handwriting to see whether the same person wrote them. Photocopiers and printers can often be identified by tiny imperfections in the copies they make, and many print almost invisible information on their printouts that police can detect. Banknotes incorporate hard-to-fake safety features, but sometimes a forgery is so good that it takes an expert forensic analyst to recognize it.

Printing and security privacy

Governments require that computer printers print a microscopic code on the pages they output, in case the police need to identify when and where a document was printed. This is especially useful for tracking documents created by criminals planning business fraud or terrorism. Office printers can inform managers over the internet whether they need repairs, paper, or ink—so it might also be possible to tell who was using a particular printer.

Micro dots

The printer's secret code is a pattern of tiny yellow dots printed across the page—best seen with a magnifying glass and under a blue light.

Coded message

This close-up from paper above shows 15 columns by eight rows of dots or gaps. When decoded, it shows the date, time, and printer ID number.

Banknote anti-forgery features

Some criminals use high-quality color photocopiers to turn out fake currency notes, which may fool people who are too busy to check them, but many features of genuine banknotes cannot be reproduced. They are printed on strong, high-quality paper or polymer, with their own characteristic "feel." The designs on a genuine banknote are extremely intricate—a photocopier may blur them. The designs on the front and back are precisely aligned—hard to do on a photocopier.

See-through register

When this note is held up to the light, the incomplete "£" symbols on the front and back combine, showing the printing coincides accurately on both sides.

Ultraviolet feature

A UV banknote-testing lamp shone onto the note makes a large "20" appear in a red and green pattern. Similar patterns appear on other parts of the note.

Watermark

A ghostly image featuring the Queen and the symbol "£20" becomes visible when held up to the light.

Holographic strip

If you turn the note to catch the light at different angles, a face or the "£" and "20" symbols appear.

Quality

Banknotes have a special feel, because of the high-quality material used—too costly for forgeries.

Microlettering

A magnifying glass reveals the note's value in tiny letters ("twenty") and numerals ("20").

Raised print

A finger run across the note can feel raised print in some areas, such as the figure "20" at bottom right.

Electrostatic detective

Forensic investigators can sometimes find traces of writing on a sheet of paper—even though they are invisible to the naked eye. When someone writes on the top sheet of a pad, a copy of the writing is left in the form of very slight impressions (dents) in the sheet beneath—or several sheets, if the writer presses hard. The ESDA (Electrostatic Detection Apparatus) is a high-tech way of making the impressions on a lower sheet visible.

1 Applying the film
The investigator lays the lower sheet of paper on a porous metal plate. A pump sucks air through the plate, pulling both paper and overlaying film hard against the plate, in order to make a good contact between them.

2 Charging the film
Waving a "wand"—a high-voltage electrode—produces an electric charge all over the film, like static. The charge is stronger where impressions in the paper create a tiny gap between it and the film.

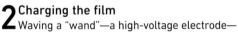

3 Scattering the toner
Powder, like a photocopier's toner, is scattered over the film, and then blown off. Some clings to the film where the charge is strongest, revealing the writing (see right).

The Dead Sea scrolls

Between 1947 and 1960, a treasure trove of Jewish religious writings was found in caves around the Dead Sea in the Middle East. Some were versions of parts of the Bible. But were they genuine? By measuring the radioactive carbon in the scrolls, carbon dating showed that the scrolls were written at various dates from the 2nd century BCE to the 1st century CE. Forgery was therefore ruled out.

Fragile scrolls fell to pieces when found.

The Führer forgeries

In 1981, a German journalist revealed he had found some diaries supposedly written by Hitler. Handwriting experts and a historian declared them authentic. But forensics experts found that the paper, inks, and binding were modern, and not available in Hitler's day. The forger and his accomplice, the journalist, were jailed.

Toner in grooves reveals writing.

Every picture tells a story

AUTHENTICITY IS KEY TO AN ARTWORK'S VALUE. Even an inferior picture by a famous artist will fetch a higher price than an excellent one by a forger. Sophisticated forensic technologies make it hard for fake paintings, statues, and other artifacts to hoodwink the experts. Forensic scientists study suspect paintings under light of various wavelengths: a forger might make a picture look convincing to the naked eye, but X-rays and infrared light do not deceive. A forger has to be extremely talented and dedicated to produce an "old" masterpiece without resorting to any modern materials.

Master forger
Tom Keating (1917–1984) claimed to have painted 2,000 forged works during his lifetime. He produced paintings in very varied styles, from the 16th century to the 20th. He claimed that he always gave clues that experts should recognize—for example, by using modern paints, or putting historical errors into scenes. Remarkably, his paintings have increased in value ever since he was exposed.

Van Meegeren painting
Investigators decided that this picture, painted in the style of the 17th-century painter Vermeer, was one of many fakes painted by the Dutch forger Han Van Meegeren. Unusually, he was desperate to prove he was guilty of forgery—not treason. After World War II (1939–1945), he was accused of having sold masterpieces to the Nazi invaders of his country. He had to paint a fake picture for the court to prove he had the skill to forge the old pictures. Although found innocent of treason, he was convicted of forgery but died in 1947, before starting his sentence.

Looking for the invisible
A powerful spotlight illuminates an oil panting with visible light (forming the bright patch on the painting) and infrared light, which is invisible radiation. The camera's thermal imaging film is sensitive to the infrared light reflected from the picture—the photograph will reveal details not visible in ordinary light, such as corrections and alterations. Infrared can also help determine whether the paint used is characteristic of a particular artist, and therefore the picture is genuine. X-rays penetrate beneath the surface of the painting to see if cracking occurs through all the layers; if it doesn't, the painting is probably a fake.

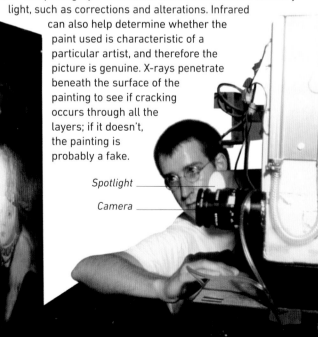

Spotlight

Camera

Cottingley fairies

Ten-year-old Frances Griffiths gazes dreamily at a troupe of fairies dancing in the garden. This photograph, taken by her 16-year-old cousin Elsie Wright in 1917, became world famous when published three years later. Many longed to believe these were real fairies. Journalists questioned the girls to find out if the pictures were faked. Using a camera lent by an expert on the paranormal, the girls produced three more pictures of fairies. Many years later, Elsie and Frances admitted that the "fairies" were paper cut-outs of pictures copied from a book.

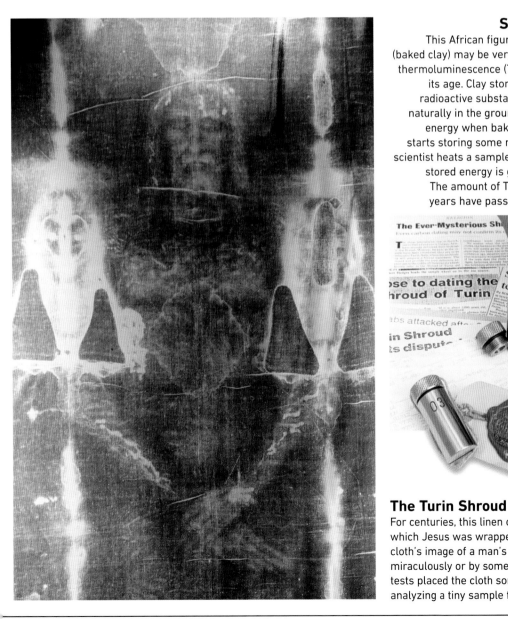

Stored energy

This African figurine in terra-cotta (baked clay) may be very old. Measuring thermoluminescence (TL) can confirm its age. Clay stores energy from radioactive substances that occur naturally in the ground, releases that energy when baked by a potter, and starts storing some more. If a forensic scientist heats a sample of the figure, the stored energy is given out as light. The amount of TL shows how many years have passed since it was made.

Shroud sample wrapped in foil

Sealed container in which sample was sent for testing

Wax seal of Archbishop of Turin

The Turin Shroud

For centuries, this linen cloth (left) was venerated as the shroud in which Jesus was wrapped when taken down from the Cross. The cloth's image of a man's body was said to have been made either miraculously or by some natural process. Three radiocarbon dating tests placed the cloth somewhere between 1260 and 1390 CE but analyzing a tiny sample from a much-handled object is problematic.

61

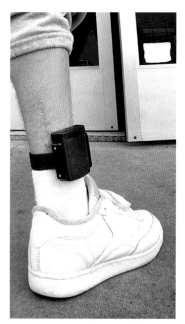

Future forensics

SCIENCE WILL OFFER AN IMPRESSIVE ARRAY of new techniques to police and forensic investigators in the near future. Advanced technology will make it easier to track suspects' movements, shopping, phone calls, and online activities. Small, handheld devices will make it speedier to detect evidence at the crime scene and even analyze it on the spot. And all of us may carry ID that can't be forged—in "biometric" details, such as facial features and eye patterns. All this means increased surveillance of our daily lives, but will make it easier to detect and solve crime.

Tracking their steps

Ankle devices give location data via GPS. These can be given to offenders to track their movements and make them stay within a given boundary—a technique called geofencing. One day, it might be possible to implant a miniature capsule under the skin that could perform the same function.

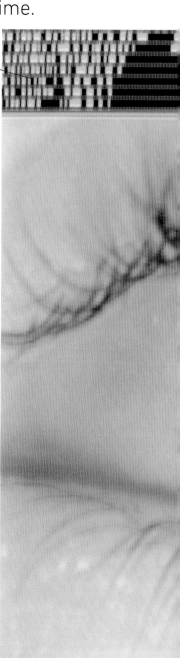

Computer converts iris details into a code

Iris scanning

This computer screen image shows the iris of an eye being scanned for personal identification. The iris is the colored area around the black central pupil and is unique in each person. To scan it, a low-power laser beam is shone into the eye. The scanner analyzes the iris by dividing it into eight circular areas to pick out details. The information about markings in each circle is broken down into a sequence of light and dark patches (see inset) and then stored as numbers in a database, where it can be matched to any existing iris profiles. It is possible to fake the iris pattern—for example, by wearing special contact lenses with an image of iris patterns printed on them. However, there are ways of detecting this kind of fraud.

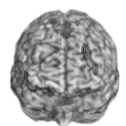

Back view

Most lying activity in frontal area

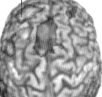

Overhead view

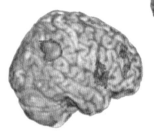

Right side

The lying brain

Functional magnetic resonance imaging (fMRI) can be used to observe how the brain works. The yellow and red areas above show brain activity during speech. The person being scanned was asked sometimes to lie and sometimes to tell the truth. One day, police may be able to use brain scans to show whether a suspect is lying.

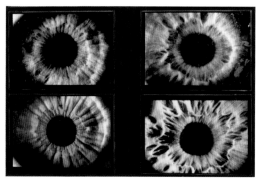

Iris types

Each iris is full of detail that is particular to each individual and more graphic than a fingerprint. A computer can analyze the iris patterns, search on a database, and make a match within just three seconds.

Mapping the face

Standard set of points measured

Face shape scanned into computer

A face can be scanned and its features summarized in a set of measurements. A mesh of lines is projected in infrared light onto a face and a computer analyzes the way the lines are curved by underlying facial features, as well as the distances between features. Facial recognition can be used as a type of security pass, for locating criminals, and is also now used as a way to access many cell phones instead of a passcode.

CCTV camera

A face in the crowd

London is thought to be the most heavily surveilled capital city in the world. Its many CCTV devices allow remote monitoring of people on stations, high streets, and other public places and many are now linked in large networks. It will be possible in the future to track a person's movements across networks or even look for a particular person if their face has already been identified. But there are concerns that such high levels of surveillance can negatively affect the privacy of the general population.

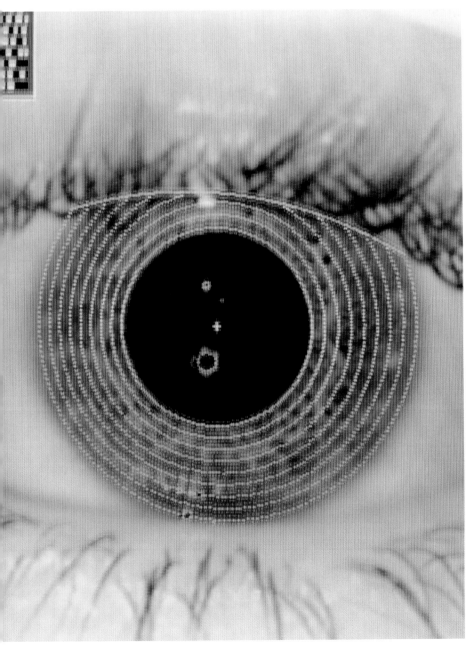

Personal profile

This scientist is examining DNA profiles. As DNA extraction techniques become ever more sensitive, even very tiny quantities of DNA left at a crime scene can be analyzed and a successful profile produced.

Hall of fame

THE MAJOR PIONEERS OF AND CONTRIBUTORS TO forensic science have come from many walks of life. Most are scientists, or police officers and detectives. Thanks to their work, forensics plays a key part in the criminal justice system.

ABAGNALE, FRANK 1948–
Having taught himself the art of fraud and forgery and starting to write checks, Abagnale ran away from home at the age of 16 and headed for New York. In a five-year crime spree, he conned banks out of more than $2.5 million while posing as an airline pilot, doctor, lawyer, and teacher.

Frank Abagnale's incredible criminal career became the subject of a film in 2002

By the time of his capture in 1969, Abagnale was wanted in 21 countries. He served less than five years in prison when the FBI released him on the condition he help them in their fight against fraud. He later founded his own security consultancy firm and became a legitimate millionaire.

BALTHAZARD, VICTOR 1872–1950
Balthazard was a professor of forensic medicine at the Sorbonne University in Paris, France. He made a comprehensive forensic study of hair, conducted research into bloodstain patterns, and used photographic enlargements of bullets and cartridge cases to determine weapon type. He was one of the first to attempt to match a bullet to a weapon.

BELL, JOSEPH 1837–1911
Dr. Bell was a lecturer at the medical school of the University of Edinburgh, Scotland, where one of his pupils was Arthur Conan Doyle. Bell had a habit of deducing a patient's occupation and history from studying his or her physical details. Conan Doyle used this trait for his fictional detective Sherlock Holmes. Bell's emphasis on close observation made him a pioneer in forensic pathology.

BERTILLON, ALPHONSE 1853–1914
French police detective and creator of anthropometry, the science of measuring the body. See pp.8–9.

BLACK, PROFESSOR DAME SUE 1961–
Known worldwide for her work in war crime and disaster victim identification (see p.7), Sue Black was Professor of Anatomy and Forensic Anthropology at the University of Dundee, Scotland, and has written several books about her work.

CRICK, FRANCIS 1916–2004
British codiscoverer—with James Watson, Maurice Wilkins, and Rosalind Franklin—of the structure of DNA. See p.22.

CRIPPEN, DR. HAWLEY HARVEY 1862–1910
American murderer captured by the use of new wireless communication. See p.40.

DNA DATABASE, 1995
The world's first DNA database was begun in Britain. It holds DNA samples of around 6 million convicted criminals and suspects. Technical advances in DNA collection and searching enable police to bring new prosecutions for previously unsolved crimes, and free those wrongly imprisoned.

FBI, 1908
The Federal Bureau of Investigation, founded in 1908 as the Bureau of Investigation, under US President Theodore Roosevelt. *See* Hoover, J. Edgar.

GALTON, SIR FRANCIS 1882–1911
Victorian polymath and author of *Fingerprinting*, which established the classification of fingerprints. See pp.18–19.

GLAISTER, SIR JOHN 1856–1932
Scottish professor of forensic medicine and expert witness. See p.20.

GODDARD, CALVIN 1891–1955
A pioneer in ballistics, Goddard headed the Bureau of Forensic Ballistics, the US's first independent crime lab, which took on fingerprinting, trace evidence, and blood analysis as well as ballistics. He advocated use of the newly invented comparison microscope to identify bullet markings, and was an expert witness at criminal trials.

GROSS, HANS 1847–1915
Gross was a magistrate and professor of criminal law at the University of Graz, Austria. His book *Criminal Investigation* explored the ways that physical evidence can be used to solve crimes.

HAUPTMANN, BRUNO 1889–1936
A German criminal who entered the US in 1923, Hauptmann lived quietly until 1935, when he was accused of the kidnapping and murder of famous aviator Charles Lindbergh's baby son. "The trial of the century" convicted Hauptmann, partly owing to similarities between his signature and a ransom note. In 2005, three independent forensic document experts confirmed he was indeed the author of the ransom note.

Hauptmann's signature

Composite signature made from ransom note

J. Edgar Hoover,
founder of the FBI

LOCARD, DR. EDMOND 1877–1966
French forensic scientist most famous for his exchange principle. See p.27.

MARSH, JAMES 1794–1896
British chemist who in 1836 devised a test for detecting arsenic, called the "Marsh test." Before the test, colorless, odorless arsenic was untraceable. The poison was used so widely to bump off family members that it became known as "inheritance powder."

ORFILA, MATHIEU 1787–1853
Born in Spain, Orfila spent most of his life in Paris, France, where he was a professor of chemistry. His *Treatise of General Toxicology* detailed new techniques for detecting arsenic in the body. This, and other works, earned Orfila the title "the father of toxicology." See p.8.

SCOTLAND YARD, 1829
Headquarters for London's Metropolitan Police, founded by Sir Robert Peel with the help of Eugène François Vidocq. The Met were early adopters of forensic science and set up the Fingerprint Branch in 1901, using the Henry System of Classification.

STARRS, JAMES E. 1930–
This American forensic anthropologist has examined the remains of more than 20 murderers in search of new evidence, including Wild West outlaw Jesse James and "Boston strangler" Albert de Salvo. Author of *A Voice for the Dead*, Starrs is a professor of law and forensic science, and edits *Scientific Sleuthing Review*.

UHLENHUTH, PAUL 1870–1957
German bacteriologist who devised a test for distinguishing blood from other liquids, and one for distinguishing human blood from other animals' blood. See p.20.

VUCETICH, JUAN 1858–1925
Argentine anthropologist and police officer, Juan Vucetich made the first prosecution based on fingerprint evidence and developed a method of fingerprint classification that would be used by police forces all over the world.

HERSCHEL, WILLIAM 1833–1918
British colonial magistrate and the first to use fingerprints for identification. See p.18.

HOOVER, J. EDGAR 1895–1972
American founder and controversial director of the FBI, Hoover held this post for 48 years. The FBI investigates crimes and gathers intelligence about potential criminal activity (see p.9). Hoover established forensics at the organization by setting up a fingerprint file, a crime lab, and the FBI National Academy for training elite officers.

WATSON, JAMES 1928–
American Nobel Prize winner and codiscoverer of DNA's structure. See p.22.

Ellis Parker (right) discusses a case with his son, Ellis Parker, Jr.

Forensic scientist James E. Starrs examines DNA sequences

JEFFREYS, SIR ALEC 1950–
British discoverer of DNA fingerprinting. See p.22.

KEATING, TOM 1917–1984
Successful British art forger. See p.60.

KGB 1917–1991
The Soviet Union's secret police used forensic science, new technology, and coercion to gather foreign intelligence and pursue the state's enemies, often to the death. When the Soviet Union was disbanded, so was the KGB.

LACASSAGNE, ALEXANDRE 1844–1921
Sometimes called the founder of forensic science, Lacassagne was a professor of forensic medicine at the University of Lyon, France, where one of his students was forensics pioneer Edmond Locard. Lacassagne was the first to study bullet markings and bloodstain pattern analysis.

LANDSTEINER, KARL 1868–1943
Austrian discoverer of ABO blood types and Nobel Prize winner. See p.20.

OSBORN, ALBERT SHERMAN 1858–1946
Author of *Questioned Documents*, Osborn analyzed forged documents for more than 50 years, and was an expert witness in many important cases. Osborn founded the American Society of Questioned Document Examiners, and designed a comparison microscope.

PARKER, ELLIS 1871–1940
Often described as America's real-life Sherlock Holmes, Parker was a Chief of Detectives in New Jersey for 45 years and helped solve more than 300 violent crimes. He used a forensic mixture of close observation, deduction, and psychology, spotting details others missed, and asking questions that often led to an important discovery.

Forensic firsts

FORENSIC SCIENCE HAS LONG BEEN a weapon in the fight against crime. Early breakthroughs included areas as diverse as medicine, optics, and handwriting analysis. This timeline tracks the most significant of those advances.

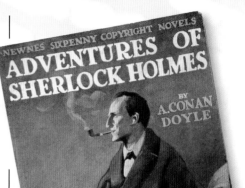

Published in 1892, this collection contained 12 of Holmes's adventures.

1247 In China, the first book on forensic science appears, called *The Washing Away of Wrongs*. Author and lawyer Sung Tz'u includes instructions on how to distinguish between suicide, murder, and natural deaths.

1609 The first study of handwriting analysis, by François Demelle, is published in France.

1642 The University of Leipzig in Germany begins a course on forensic medicine.

1670 The first powerful precision microscope is invented by Dutch scientist Anton van Leeuwenhoek.

1776 During the American Revolution, the corpse of General Warren is identified by his false tooth, made from a walrus tusk.

1794 British murderer John Toms is convicted on the basis of a torn scrap of paper found on his victim that matched a piece in Toms' pocket.

1804 German physicist Johann Wilhelm Ritter discovers ultraviolet radiation, which will be used to reveal trace evidence that is invisible in normal light.

Early precision microscope

1812 The world's first detective force, the Sûreté Nationale, is established in Paris, France. It becomes a model for Britain's Scotland Yard and the US's FBI.

1813 The influential book *Treatise of Toxicology* by Spanish doctor Mathieu Orfila is published.

1823 Czech anatomist Johann Evangelista Purkinje describes fingerprint types.

1828 Scottish physicist William Nicol invents the polarizing light microscope, which will help detect trace evidence.

1835 British police officer Henry Goddard studies bullet markings and demonstrates these can be used to match a bullet to the gun that fired it.

1836 British chemist James Marsh devises a test for detecting minute quantities of arsenic in the body. The test is soon used successfully in murder trials.

1841 The first detective story, *The Murders in the Rue Morgue* by American author Edgar Allen Poe, is published. From now on, developments in forensic science will be reflected in the work of fictional detectives.

1843 The first mug shots of suspects are taken by police in Brussels, Belgium.

1850 In the US, murderer John Webster is the first to be convicted by medical evidence, when doctors determine the age, sex, and time of death of his victim.

1856 In India, administrative officer Sir William Herschel begins to use thumb-prints on documents to identify illiterates.

1859 The US becomes the first country to allow photographs to be used as evidence in courts of law.

1861 German professor of pathological anatomy Rudolph Virchow makes a study of the value of hair as physical evidence.

1878 The Criminal Investigation Department (CID) is Britain's first plain-clothes detective force. The CID is controlled by Scotland Yard.

1880s Italian criminologist Cesare Lombroso measures changes in blood volume to discover if any physiological changes are associated with lying.

1882 Anthropometry, a system of bodily measurements, starts to be used as a means of identifying criminals in Paris, France. It will be used by police forces all over the world.

1887 Arthur Conan Doyle's *A Study in Scarlet,* the first story featuring Sherlock Holmes, is published in the UK. Holmes goes on to appear in four novels and 56 short stories and become the world's most popular fictional detective.

1891 Argentinian police officer Juan Vucetich makes the first criminal identification using fingerprints. As a result, a murderer is convicted. The following year, the Argentinian police force becomes the world's first to use fingerprinting as a means of criminal identification.

1892 *Fingerprints,* by British scientist Francis Galton, is published. The book establishes a classification system, and shows that fingerprints are not inherited, and that even the prints of identical twins are different.

1893 The book *System der Kriminalistik* by German forensic scientist Hans Gross covers microscopy, serology, fingerprints, and ballistics. It appears in English in 1907 as *Criminal Investigation*.

1894 In France, Captain Alfred Dreyfus is wrongly convicted of treason by an incorrect handwriting identification by expert Alphonse Bertillon. The scandal rocks French politics.

1895 German physicist Wilhelm Conrad Röntgen discovers X-rays, which will earn him a Nobel Prize in Physics. X-rays will become a key tool for forensic anthropologists and odontologists.

1896 In Britain, Sir Edward Richard Henry publishes *Classification and Uses of Fingerprints,* establishing a fingerprint classification system that will come to be used across Europe and North America.

1898 German chemist Paul Jeserich gets a killer convicted by firing a bullet from a suspect's gun and matching it with one from the crime scene.

1901 Austrian pathologist Karl Landsteiner demonstrates three blood types, leading to the ABO system of blood typing.

1901 German scientist Paul Uhlenhuth devises the precipitin test to distinguish human blood from that of other animals.

1902 Burglar Harry Jackson is the first person in the UK to be convicted by fingerprint evidence.

1904 In Germany, the precipitin test is first used in a criminal court, to convict brutal murderer Ludwig Tessnow.

1910 *Questioned Documents* by American document examiner and handwriting expert Albert Osborn is published. The book is still consulted by experts today.

1910 The world's first forensic laboratory is opened in France by Edmond Locard.

1911 Murderer Thomas Jennings is hanged after being convicted by fingerprint evidence in Chicago.

A record of a suspect's fingerprints

1913 Victor Balthazard, professor of forensic medicine at the University of Sorbonne, Paris, details how bullet markings make every bullet unique.

1916 In the US, detective Albert Schneider uses a vacuum apparatus to collect trace evidence.

1920 French forensic expert Edmond Locard formulates his exchange principle, usually summarized as "every contact leaves a trace."

1920 An international catalog of firearms is begun by Charles E. Thwaite in the US. Five years later, the collection is complete and any bullet can be matched to the gun that fired it.

1920 Physicist John Fisher invents a device called a helixometer, for recording the interiors of gun barrels.

1920 American Luke May is the first to study how striation marks on tools can be compared and used as evidence.

1920 *The Mysterious Affair at Styles* is published in the US. Agatha Christie's first novel introduces the Belgian detective Hercule Poirot. He will feature in 33 novels and 54 short stories, and in many films.

1921 The first lie detector test, or polygraph, is invented by John Larson in the US. The machine measures blood pressure and rate of breathing.

1923 The US's first independent crime laboratory, The Bureau of Forensic Ballistics, opens for business.

1924 In the US, two killers are convicted when experts showed that one of them owned the typewriter used to write a ransom note.

1924 Los Angeles Chief of Police August Vollmer opens the US's first police crime laboratory.

1925 The first comparison microscope, important for matching bullet and other markings, is invented in the US by Philip Gravelle and Calvin Goddard.

1926 In the US, Italian-born laborers Nicola Sacco and Bartolomeo Vanzetti are convicted for robbery and murder, largely by ballistics evidence from the new comparison microscope.

1929 In Chicago, one of the hit men responsible for gunning down seven mobsters in the St. Valentine's Day Massacre is identified when guns at his home are matched to cartridge cases from the crime scene.

1930s Mexico introduces the first test to identify gunshot residue on skin, the dermal nitrate test.

The presence of maggots can help determine time of death.

1930 In the US, the National Fingerprint File is started by the FBI.

1930 *The American Journal of Police Science* is founded and published by staff of the Bureau of Forensic Ballistics.

1932 The FBI opens its own crime lab, the Technical Crime Laboratory.

1936 In a murder trial, Scottish doctor Alexander Mearns uses the life cycle of maggots to estimate the time of the victim's death.

1936 Handwriting evidence helps convict German-born murderer Bruno Hauptmann in the US.

1941 The voice spectrograph is invented by researchers at Bell Laboratories in the US. The device is intended to identify suspects from speech characteristics.

1948 The American Academy of Forensic Sciences (AAFS) is founded to bring together forensic scientists working in different disciplines.

1950 Tape lift method of collecting trace evidence is developed by Swiss criminalist Max Frei-Sulzer.

1953 Cambridge scientists James Crick and Francis Watson announce that they have discovered the double-helix structure of DNA.

1954 The Breathalyzer, which estimates alcohol content in the blood, is invented by Robert Borkenstein in the US. The device will be adopted by police departments around the world.

1959 A color test for detecting gunshot residue by its metallic elements is developed in the US. It is named the Harrison–Gilroy test after its inventors.

1965 In Britain, a team at Cambridge University develops the first scanning electron microscope (SEM). SEMs produce high-resolution 3-D images for analyzing samples in incredible detail.

1967 In the US, the FBI opens the National Crime Information Center to coordinate information about criminals and stolen goods.

1971 French photographer Jacques Penry creates the Photo-FIT ID System, capable of creating 15 billion different faces.

1975 The FBI introduces the Automated Fingerprint Identification System (AFIS).

Fibers in a needle's eye, as seen by a scanning electron microscope

1977 In Japan, trace evidence examiner Masato Soba discovers superglue fuming. This is a method of revealing latent (hidden) fingerprints.

1978 The electrostatic detection apparatus (ESDA) is invented by British scientists Bob Freeman and Doug Foster. It reveals impressions of handwriting in paper.

1983 The Hitler Diaries, bought by the German news magazine *Stern*, are shown to be fake by forensic document examiners.

1984 British geneticist Sir Alec Jeffreys discovers DNA fingerprinting, which uses variations in the genetic code to identify an individual.

1986 Polymerase Chain Reaction (PCR), a method of duplicating parts of the DNA molecule, is developed by chemist Kary Mullis in the US, enabling identifications to be made from a minute sample of DNA.

1988 In Britain, DNA fingerprinting is used to solve a crime for the first time. It exonerates a murder suspect, and then it nails the real culprit, Colin Pitchfork.

1989 In the US, Gary Dotson becomes the first person to have a conviction overturned by DNA evidence.

1991 University College Hospital, London, develops a laser scanning technique that enables a computer simulation of a human face based on the skull's shape.

1992 The FBI launches Drugfire, a firearms identification database which stores details of markings for search and comparison to find out if crimes were committed using the same weapons.

1993 The remains of the last Russian czar, Nicholas II, and his family are positively identified 75 years after their assassination by comparing samples of DNA from bone tissue with close relatives.

1994 The UK Home Office publishes a report called *CCTV: Looking Out For You*, which paves the way for a huge increase in the use of Closed Circuit Television cameras in public places.

1995 The world's first DNA database, containing DNA records of convicted criminals, is set up in the UK. Other countries soon follow suit.

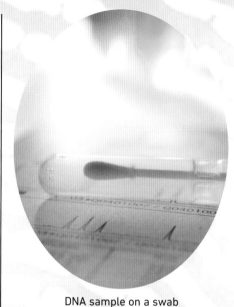

DNA sample on a swab

1998 In the US, professor Don Foster helps police find serial bomber Ted Kaczynski through the new forensic science of literary analysis—studying documents the killer had written to discover who and where he was.

1999 The National Integrated Ballistics Information Network replaces the FBI's Drugfire database. It is an automated computer network containing digital images of ballistics evidence.

1999 The AFIS is integrated to create the Integrated Automated Fingerprint Identification System, making searching for matches much faster.

2000 The first episode of *CSI: Crime Scene Investigation* is broadcast on TV in the US. The program shows crimes being solved entirely by a team of forensic investigators. *CSI* is a huge hit worldwide, and many other dramas about forensic science soon follow.

2001 Toxicologists examine a lock of hair that belonged to the French emperor Napoleon I, who died in 1821. It reveals that he suffered from long-term arsenic poisoning, which may have killed him.

2006 Developed in the UK, Automated Number Plate Recognition (ANPR) systems can now scan license plates at around one per second on vehicles traveling up to 100 mph (160 km/h), and can check a registered number on a database of stored license plates to identify the vehicle's owner.

2011 Virtopsies (virtual autopsies), which are 3-D images built from CT (computed tomography) scans and MRI (magnetic resonance imaging), are used to find cause of death and as evidence of a crime.

Find out more

FORENSIC SCIENCE THRILLS countless readers and TV audiences, but it is getting interactive, too, online and in museum exhibitions. For budding forensic scientists, there are plenty of opportunities to explore this fascinating subject.

USEFUL WEBSITES

- This US homeschooling site has a section about forensic science, with links to various activities **https://a2zhomeschooling.com/explore/chemistry_kids/csi_unit_study_forensics_for_kids/**
- *CSI: The Experience—Web Adventures* has various games and activities based on the TV series **http://forensics.rice.edu/en/For-Educators/Online-Activities.html**
- Explore forensic anthropology with 17th-century bone biographies **https://naturalhistory.si.edu/education/teaching-resources/written-bone**
- Read about Vancouver's history of crime, policing, and justice **https://vancouverpolicemuseum.ca/**
- Sydney's Justice and Police Museum tells the stories of notorious criminals and remarkable police officers **https://sydneylivingmuseums.com.au/justice-police-museum/stories**
- Learn more about the science behind solving crime at the Science Museum **https://www.sciencemuseum.org.uk**

Display at the Vancouver Police Museum

Forensics on show

As well as specialist crime and forensics museums, such as the Police Museum in Vancouver, Canada, science museums have temporary shows on forensic technology.

Police officer and K-9, from Nebraska State Patrol, with local schoolchildren

Police at school

Police officers visit schools to tell pupils about the role of the police in their community, and provide advice on keeping safe and asking for help when needed.

A museum guard dressed as a Victorian "bobby"

Museum of detection

In London's Baker Street, the Sherlock Holmes Museum pays tribute to the fictional master of deductive reasoning. The famous study is kept exactly as it is described in the stories.

Glossary

ACCELERANT A highly flammable substance that can be used to start a fire, such as gasoline.

ANTHROPOMETRY A system of body measurements once used by police forces for identification.

A bullet hole in reinforced glass leaves a clear record for the ballistics investigator

ARSON The crime of starting a fire deliberately in order to cause damage to property.

AUTOPSY A medical examination of a corpse in order to discover the cause of death. Also known as a post-mortem.

BALLISTICS In forensic science ballistics means the study of guns, bullets, and trajectories.

BLACK BOX An event recorder, fitted to planes, ships, and trains, that holds instrument and voice recordings.

BLOOD TYPE Everyone belongs to one of four main blood types: A, B, AB, or O.

CALIBER A measure of the inside diameter of a gun's barrel, given in inches, hundredths of inches, or millimeters.

CARTRIDGE CASE A cylinder containing the explosive charge and bullet or pellets for a gun.

CAUSE OF DEATH The action that resulted in death (such as a blow to the head), as distinct from a medical condition (such as brain hemorrhage).

CHAIN OF CUSTODY The trail followed from crime scene to court by a piece of evidence held by the police and forensic scientists. Written records must show who passed the evidence to whom and when.

CHROMATOGRAPHY A series of laboratory tests designed to separate out the components of a mixture. In forensic science, chromatographic tests are used to discover the presence of drugs or poisons.

CLEANSUIT Outfit worn by forensic investigators at crime scene, designed to prevent contamination.

COMPARATOR A device that enlarges and projects images of two different fingerprints for easy comparison.

COMPARISON MICROSCOPE A double microscope for examining two similar items, often bullets, side by side.

COMPUTER TOMOGRAPHY (CT) A method of X-raying the body in sections and creating three-dimensional images of its parts.

CONTAMINATION The transfer of material to or from another source by physical contact that compromises evidence, whether unwittingly or maliciously.

DATABASE An organized collection of information—such as DNA, fingerprints, or firearms—usually computerized for quick and easy searching.

DUSTING Brushing for latent fingerprints with a powder to make them visible.

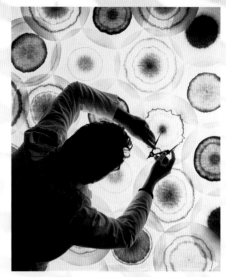
Scientist examining paper chromatograms

E-FIT SYSTEM Computerized photographic identification system using phots of facial features to create a likeness of a suspect. A similar system called FACES exists in the United States.

ELECTROPHORESIS Analytical method using an electric charge to grade substances by size and, in the case of DNA samples, generate DNA profiles.

ELECTROSTATIC DETECTION APPARATUS (ESDA) A device that reveals handwriting impressions on paper.

ENTOMOLOGY The study of insects. A forensic entomologist studies the life cycles of insects found on corpses as an aid to estimating time of death.

FIBER EVIDENCE Evidence provided by human and animal hairs, or by synthetic fibers.

DNA—THE LADDER OF LIFE

Inside the nuclei of the cells that make up every part of the body is a molecule called deoxyribonucleic acid, or DNA. It is a microscopic map of a person's unique features and characteristics, and a set of instructions for their development. DNA is composed of two strands that twist around each other in a double helix. The two strands are linked by rungs, which are composed of four chemicals, shown here in different colors. It is the order of these chemical rungs that is different in every person—only identical twins, triplets, and so on share the same DNA.

Model of the DNA double helix

Each rung is composed of two chemicals.

DNA strand is an incredible 6 ft (2 m) long.

FINGERTIP SEARCH
A crime scene search carried out by several police officers kneeling shoulder-to-shoulder.

FORENSIC ANTHROPOLOGY
The study of skeletons for identification.

GUNSHOT RESIDUE (GSR) Microscopic powder from explosive that is sprayed onto the hand of a person firing a gun. It is invisible, but can be detected with a hand swab up to six hours after firing.

HOMICIDE The act of killing an individual. Can be manslaughter or murder.

LARVA A stage in the development of an insect before it undergoes metamorphosis into its adult form. When larvae are found on a corpse, knowledge of their life cycle can help indicate time of death.

LASER BEAM An intense beam of monochromatic light. May be used at a crime scene to trace a bullet's trajectory.

LATENT FINGERPRINT One that is not visible to the naked eye and requires special techniques to make it clear.

LIE DETECTOR *See* Polygraph.

LINEN TESTER An alternative magnifying glass often used by forensic investigators.

LOCARD'S EXCHANGE PRINCIPLE The principle behind trace evidence collection and analysis—"every contact leaves a trace"—formulated by Edmond Locard.

LUMINOL A chemical spray used to reveal traces of blood.

MAGNETIC WAND Used in conjunction with magnetic powder to dust for fingerprints on glossy surfaces.

MASS SPECTROMETRY A technique used to discover the exact quantity of drugs in a sample and detect accelerants.

MORTUARY Also called a morgue, this is the place where dead bodies are kept before a funeral.

ODONTOLOGY Forensic dentistry. Usually involves making identifications from bite marks, or from matching a body's teeth to dental records.

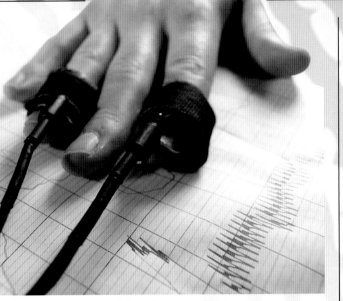
Polygraph or lie detector test

PATHOLOGY The study of diseases from body tissue. A forensic pathologist applies this study to investigating suspicious deaths and seeks to discover the cause of death by carrying out an autopsy.

PATTERN EVIDENCE Evidence that is significant for its shape or pattern. Typically bloodstains, which are classified in six different patterns.

POLYGRAPH Also known as a lie detector, an instrument designed to discover whether a person is lying by recording changes in blood pressure and pulse.

POLYMERASE CHAIN REACTION (PCR) A method of duplicating fragments of DNA until there is enough for DNA profiling or other analysis.

POST-MORTEM INTERVAL Estimated time since death. The term *post-mortem* is Latin for "after death" and can also refer to an autopsy.

PRECIPITIN TEST A test to distinguish human from animal blood.

PRESUMPTIVE TEST A test, most commonly the Kastle-Meyer test, to show quickly whether a liquid is blood and therefore requires more detailed analysis.

PROVENANCE A record of an object's history, including its origin and all its owners. Important for art and antiquities, provenance can be faked by forgers.

RIFLING The raised, spiraling pattern in a gun barrel, which can cause distinctive marks on bullets.

RIGOR MORTIS The stiffness of a corpse that occurs some hours after death. It

can help investigators determine time of death.

SCANNING ELECTRON MICROSCOPE (SEM) A powerful microscope that uses a beam of electrons instead of light to magnify an image.

SEARCH PATTERN An organized method of searching a crime scene. There are many different search patterns.

SEROLOGY The study of blood and other body fluids, usually for purposes of identification.

SNIFFER DOG A dog that has been trained to use its sensitive sense of smell to detect explosives, illegal drugs, missing people—or even corpses. "Cadaver dogs" specialize in finding human remains.

SUSPECT Someone who may be involved in a crime but has not been formally charged.

TAPE LIFT A method for recovering trace evidence—such as gunshot residue, fibers, or fingerprints—from a surface, using adhesive tape.

TOOL MARK Mark on a surface from which investigators may be able to identify the type of tool that made it, or even the individual tool—evidence which may in turn lead to the criminal who used it.

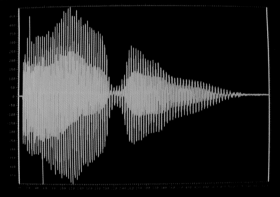
Voiceprint of a two-syllable word

TOXICOLOGY The study of drugs and poisons.

TRACE EVIDENCE Small objects or small amounts of substances that can be used as evidence—typically hair, fibers, or soil, transferred unknowingly by contact.

VOICEPRINT Graphic representation of the sound of an individual's speech patterns, which may be used for identification.

X-RAY A type of electromagnetic radiation that penetrates soft tissue and is used to scan and create images of bones.

Index

Acknowledgments

Dorling Kindersley would like to thank London South Bank University for allowing its forensic equipment to be photographed, and the following for their kind assistance:

Saul Carrol, Steve Jones, Sophie Park, & Emma Payne; Peter Winfield for illustrations 11br, 32bc; Sarah Smithies and Aditya Katyal for picture research; Steve Setford for editing; Rebecca Painter & Carey Scott for the reference pages; Hilary Bird for the index; Jim Green and Carey Scott for the wallchart; Priyanka Bansal, Rakesh Kumar, and Saloni Singh for the jacket.

The publisher would also like to thank the following for their kind permission to reproduce their photographs:

(Key: a-above; b-below/bottom; c-center; f-far; l-left; r-right; t-top)

Alamy Stock Photo: Si Barber 29tl; John Boykin 47br; chris brignell 4cra; chris brignell 14clb; Scott Camazine 36crb; Jon Challicom 54bl; Richard Gardner 25cra; Chris Gomersall 40tr;

GOwst 69br; Mikael Karlsson 69bl; Ellen McKnight 27b; Ian Miles-Flashpoint Pictures 13cl, 13tl; Pablo Paul 12c, 28c; Pictorial Press Ltd 56tl; Monty Rakusen 25b; Adrian Sherratt 57cl; Igor Stevanovic 45br/display; Westend61 GmbH / Andrew Brookes 63crb; Gari Wyn Williams 13ca; Doug Wilson 52cl; Xinhua 69c; ZUMA Press, Inc. 62tl; Ardea: Pascal Goetgheluck 37cl; Steve Hopkin 36tr, 37bc, 37cr, 37t; CEPHOS Corporation: 62bl; Corbis: 8cr, 31tr, 47cr; Lewis Allen 6tr; Morton Beebe 37br; Annebicque Bernard 23br; Bettmann 20tr, 27tr, 31tl, 33bl, 47tl, 64-65br, 65t; Régis Bossu/Sygma 53br; Andrew Brookes 68r; Richard Chung/Reuters 19br; John Mc Coy 7tr; P. Deliss/Godong 61; Kieran Doherty/Reuters 56cla; epa 49r; FDNY/Assignment ID: 30039450A 48tr; Federal Bureau of Investigation/epa 46l; Laurence Fordyce/Eye Ubiquitous 40tl; Hulton-Deutsch Collection 8cra, 40br; Nadeem Khawer/epa 55br; Micro Discovery 68l; Richard T. Nowitz 65b; Sebastian Pfuetze/zefa 7tl; Matt Rainey/ Star Ledger 7cl; Reuters 40bl, 40c, 41, 52-53tl, 54c, 54cr, 54tr, Scotland Yard/Reuters 45bl; Sion

Touhig 54-55tc; West Semitic Research/Dead Sea Scrolls Foundation 59tr; Tim Wright 52bl; Courtesy of The Bank of England: 58b; The Design Works, Sheffield: 38cl, 38cr, 38tc, 38tl, 38tr; DK Images: Courtesy of HM Customs and Excise 4fcl, 34ca; Courtesy of the Metropolitan Police Museum, London 4cl, 8-9ca, 8-9t, 9tr; Dr Thomas Heseltine/ Aurora CS Ltd: 63tl; Dr Thomas Heseltine 44br; Dreamstime.com: Felipe Caparros Cruz 57tl; Piyamas Dulmunsumphun 56crb; Fad1986 57tr; Aleksandr Matveev 45br/Oscilloscope; The Electronic Frontier Foundation: 58tr; Environmental Criminology Research Inc.: 46cra, 46tr; Faro UK: Neil Barnett 43cl; Firearmsid.com: 31br; www.firetactics.com: 48b; Foster+Freeman: 19cb, 24br, 28br; Getty Images: Corbis News / Mike Kemp 63tr; Jeff J Mitchell 7bc; Los Angeles Times / Kari Rene Hall 48cr; iStockphoto.com: E+ / Steve Debenport 47tl; The Kobal Collection: CBS-TV 7cr; Dreamworks 64-65l; Universal 9bl; LAKEHEAD UNIVERSITY INSTRUMENTATION LABORATORY, THUNDER BAY, ON CANADA: 27cr; Leeds Precision Instruments, Inc.: 33t; Mary Evans Picture Library: 48br; Chris Coupland 66t; Missouri State Police Crime Laboratory: PA Photos: 10-11b, 11ca, 11cl, 11cr, 34tr, 34-35b, 35tl, 39br, 41bl, 42c, 42tl, 42tr, 60l; Gareth Copley 35c; Ian Nicholson/PA Archive 30tl;

Photo courtesy of Sirchie: 19t; Photoshot: UPPA 20cl; Reuters: John Sommers II 35tc; Rex Features: 55bc, 55cl; Science Photo Library: A. Barrington Brown 22cl; Dr Tony Brain 26bl; Dr Jeremy Burgess 70l; CNRI 42cr; Michael Donne 49t; Mauro Fermariello 24tl, 29r; E. Gueho 26crb; James King-Holmes 61bc, 62-63b; Mark Maio/ King-Holmes 62br; Peter Menzel 6-7bl; Hank Morgan 71b; Louise Murray 35br; Susumu Nishinaga 26br; David Parker 22bl; Pasieka 66-67 (Background), 68-69 (Backdrop), 68-69 (Background), 70-71 (Background); Philippe Psaila 33br, 33cl, 33cr; David R.Frazier 16tr; David Scharf 26clb; Science Source 67b; Volker Steger 60b; Tek Image 20c, 71t; Geoff Tompkinson 70tr; Volker Steger, Peter Arnold Inc. 24tr; Shutterstock: Andrey Svytsky 24c; www.skullsunlimited.com: 2cr, 42bl, 42cl, 42clb; TopFoto.co.uk: 9c, 60t, 65c; Fortean 61t; VisionMetric Ltd: www.visionmetric. com 45tl, 45cr, 45clb; The Wellcome Institute Library, London: 8bc, 8c, 8fcl; Susan Moberly: 23bc; Jerry Young: 43t

All other images © Dorling Kindersley
For further information see: www.dkimages.com